Carthage

A Captivating Guide to the Carthaginian Empire and Its Conflicts with the Ancient Greek City-States and the Roman Republic in the Sicilian Wars and Punic Wars

Free Bonus from Captivating History
(Available for a Limited time)

Hi History Lovers!

Now you have a chance to join our exclusive history list so you can get your first history ebook for free as well as discounts and a potential to get more history books for free! Simply visit the link below to join.

Captivatinghistory.com/ebook

Also, make sure to follow us on Facebook, Twitter and Youtube by searching for Captivating History.

Contents

FREE BONUS FROM CAPTIVATING HISTORY (AVAILABLE FOR A LIMITED TIME) 1

INTRODUCTION 3

CHAPTER 1 – A NEW CITY IN THE WEST 5

CHAPTER 2 – BECOMING A MEDITERRANEAN POWER 14

CHAPTER 3 – FIGHTING FOR CONTROL OVER SICILY 23

CHAPTER 4 – FROM ALLIES TO ENEMIES 40

CHAPTER 5 – REVITALIZATION AND DEMISE 56

CHAPTER 6 – SUCCUMBING TO THE WOUNDS 75

CHAPTER 7 – THE CARTHAGINIAN SOCIETY AND GOVERNMENT ... 85

CHAPTER 8 – ARMY OF THE CARTHAGINIAN REPUBLIC 98

CHAPTER 9 – THE PUNIC CIVILIZATION 109

CONCLUSION 120

BIBLIOGRAPHY 122

FREE BONUS FROM CAPTIVATING HISTORY (AVAILABLE FOR A LIMITED TIME) 124

Introduction

Very few of the ancient empires and nations were able to challenge the Romans, who were famous for their military might and later on became a vast empire. Even fewer were able to make them shiver just by mentioning their name. In fact, only one enemy of Rome managed to engrave such fear into their bones. That was Carthage, sometimes called the Carthaginian Empire. It was a formidable state that stretched across northern Africa, from Algeria and Tunisia to the shores of Morocco and southern Spain. In its heyday, it was a formidable force that controlled much of the western Mediterranean. As such, it was the first real obstacle to the rise of the Roman state, the only one which almost brought it down before it even became an ancient superpower. Hannibal Barca, the most famous Carthaginian leader, was at one point in front of the gates of Rome. Because of that, the Carthaginian Empire, usually personified by Hannibal himself, is typically seen and described as the great foe of Rome, one of the rare daunting opponents the Romans faced.

However, despite the truth behind such sentiments, Carthage was much more than just an enemy of Rome. It was a thriving state, with its own culture and way of life. Its people were more than just soldiers. Among them were merchants, artists, artisans, priests, farmers, and much more. They built temples and palaces, houses and markets, and they erected entire cities across their not-so-small empire. In fact, behind the visage of Carthage as the adversary of the Romans lays an entire civilization worthy of our attention. Uncovering it from the shrouded veils of the past will not only help us understand Carthage itself, as well as its conflicts with Rome, but it will also give us a better comprehension of the ancient world as a whole. This guide will try to do precisely that, paint both sides of the coin that is the Carthaginian Empire, hopefully sparking your interest to find out more about both Carthage and history in general.

Chapter 1 – A New City in the West

The story of Carthage, one of the ancient jewels of the west, begins on the other side of the Mediterranean Sea in the 2nd millennium BCE. On its eastern shores, in the region known as the Levant, which is roughly the equivalent of modern-day Syria, Lebanon, Jordan, Israel, and Palestine, lived a large group of people that we call today the Canaanites. That is a modern reading of *Kn'nm*, which is what they called themselves. However, these people, despite speaking a quite similar language, were not united into a single state. Instead, they mostly lived in small city-states, like the ancient Greeks. Among them was a smaller distinct tribe, a nation of sorts, which was called Phoenicia by the ancient Greeks. It is among them that the tale of the Carthaginians has its roots.

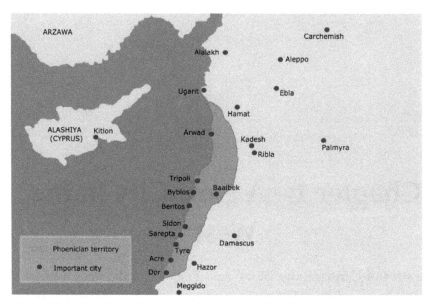

Map of Phoenician lands. Source: https://commons.wikimedia.org

What separated the Phoenicians from other Canaanites was the fact that since around 1500 BCE, their primary profession was trade. In an era where the ancient Greeks were still to find how fruitful commerce could be, Phoenician merchants roamed across the eastern Mediterranean. Their location helped them to thrive in that, as they lived mostly in what is today Lebanon. In ancient times, it was an important crossroads, connecting Mesopotamia, Egypt, Asia Minor, and Greece. However, despite their riches, the Phoenicians never created an empire, and, like the other Canaanites, they never united into a single state. Yet their city-states, among which the most important were Sidon, Byblos, and Tyre, were wealthy and powerful enough to start spreading across the Mediterranean, creating colonies as far as Spain. Some of the earliest Phoenician colonies were dated to around 1100 BCE, centuries before the Greeks began their wave of colonization. However, these dates remain debated among historians. Like the Greeks, the Phoenicians weren't trying to conquer new lands and create empires as much as they wanted to expand their trade network and access to tradable goods.

6

By the 10th century BCE, Phoenician colonization picked up the pace, and dozens of new cities spawned from Tunisia to Spain. The new colonies were so prosperous that it wasn't long before they grew from trade settlements into urban centers, helped by the fact that the local indigenous population was far behind in civilizational development. The majority of them were formed by the city of Tyre, which became the leading Phoenician city-state, as it was the wealthiest and most powerful. However, its power wasn't measured with a large army, as the Phoenicians were never really interested in waging wars. Thus, when the Neo-Assyrian Empire began expanding outside Mesopotamia, the Phoenician treasure wasn't enough to keep them out of harm's way, and by the mid-9th century BCE, they began sending tributes to the Assyrians. This marked the slow downfall of the Phoenician cities, though they were still not fully conquered. Despite spiraling downward, Tyre was still capable of founding new cities in the late 9th century. Fate would have it that one of the last colonies to be established by this city-state would grow to eclipse not only its founder but also the entire Phoenician nation.

The newly established settlement was aptly named "the new city," *Qart-hadasht* in the Phoenician language, as it was in the vicinity of an earlier colony called Utica. The name was later transcribed as *Carchedon* by the Greeks. As with many other things, the Romans appropriated the Hellenized version, calling that city *Carthago*, which is very similar to the name we use today. According to mythological histories left to us by the ancient writers, the town was founded around 814 BCE by Elishat (often Hellenized into Ellisa). Later on, she became known by the name Dido, meaning beloved in Phoenician. She was the sister of the Tyre king Pygmalion, who, according to most of the myths, cheated her from the shared rule by killing her husband. The exact details of his transgression differ in various versions of the legend. Still, they all lead to Dido leaving the city, sailing to the west. According to one of the stories, on her way to North Africa, Dido and her followers stopped at the Phoenician colonies on Cyprus. There, she saved eighty virgins from ritual prostitution and was joined by a priest of Baal, the Phoenician god equivalent to Zeus or Jupiter. With this enlarged fellowship, Dido proceeded toward what is today Tunisia.

Upon their arrival in Africa, the queen and her followers encountered both the indigenous population, known to us as Berbers and Libyans to the Romans, as well as the Phoenician colonists from Utica. The ancient writers tell us that both groups welcomed Dido without hostility. The Berbers were reportedly interested in trade and mutually beneficial dealings. Still, they wouldn't just give up their land to the newcomers. Their king welcomed them but allowed the queen and her followers to stay only on the land a single ox hide could cover. In response, Dido cut the hide into strips and enclosed the hill of Byrsa with it, which would become the citadel of Carthage. The king accepted this but imposed a yearly rent. At the same time, the Phoenicians from Utica helped their brethren through trade. The newly founded city prospered quickly due to its favorable position, which, according to myths, led to numerous suitors asking for Dido's hand. Yet she refused them all, in respect of her late husband. Most of the stories end with her throwing herself onto a funeral pyre either because she is forced to marry a local Berber king or because the Trojan hero Aeneas refuses to marry her and sails away to Italy.

Late ancient illustration of Dido's death as she sets her own funeral pyre ablaze.
Source: https://commons.wikimedia.org

However, the myth of Carthage's founding, despite its thrilling narrative, is considered to be mostly a folktale by modern historians. First of all, all the surviving versions come from Roman or Greek writers who lived centuries after the supposed event, as there are no surviving records written by the Carthaginians. That fact is true for all written accounts of Carthage's history, which is especially troublesome as both the Greeks and the Romans were at one point its adversaries. Further complicating the issue is the fact that most of those writers lived after the fall of Carthage and were mostly interested in contacts and dealings between the Carthaginians and other nations. Archeology can do little to help in this matter for two reasons. First is the fact that the site of Carthage is still inhabited, limiting the possibility of significant research. Secondly, few inscriptions and engravings written in Punic, the language of the Carthaginians, that can be found are hard to interpret. Modern knowledge has a partial understanding of the Punic language, so the exact meaning of the words is debated among scholars. Despite that, archeological findings in recent decades are crucial for our understanding of Carthage, giving us a clearer and fuller picture of its history.

That being said, historians and archeologists have found evidence that confirms parts of Dido's myth. Several objects found at the site of Carthage have confirmed the first Phoenician settlement was founded in the second half of the 9th century or very early 8th century, which is when most ancient writers date the arrival of Dido in Africa. Furthermore, a golden locket was found with inscriptions that mention King Pygmalion of Tyre. Historians are still debating if the locket and the other objects were correctly dated, though. Thus, it is quite probable that the city of Tyre indeed founded Carthage in the period mentioned. When it comes to the question of Dido herself, historians tend to believe she, like her brother, was a real person. The reason behind this is the fact that women in founding myths are rare in ancient times, as they were usually seen as somewhat lesser than men. Additionally, the legends aren't proclaiming her to be of some divine or heroic ancestry, which would've given Carthage a propaganda point in ancient times. Therefore, the Carthaginians wouldn't have gained anything from inventing such a character as their founder. Later practices of Carthaginians sending gifts to a temple in Tyre and to the local Berber population corroborate the likelihood of Dido's founding myth to be based on reality to a certain degree. However, it definitely should not be taken as entirely factual.

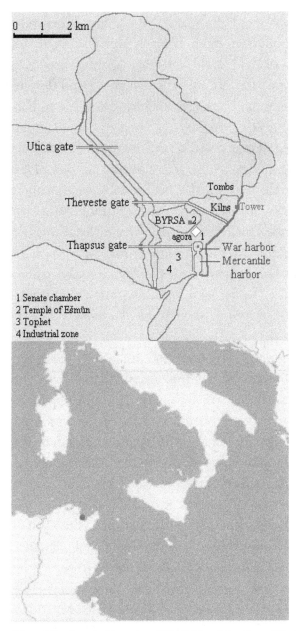

Plan of Carthage in 2ᵈ century BCE (left) and location of Carthage (right).
Source: https://commons.wikimedia.org

Regardless of the founding myth, whoever chose the location of the New City selected an unusually favorable position. Locally, the settlement was erected on an arrow-shaped peninsula in the Gulf of

Tunis. The citadel on the Byrsa Hill overlooked the shores beneath, providing decent protection from both the sea and land. On the northern half of the peninsula laid fertile lands that were first used as a food source but later became the city suburbs as it grew. And despite not having a river near them, the Carthaginians had freshwater springs capable of servicing their needs. Moreover, Carthage was also quite well connected. The Gulf of Tunis provided calmer waters needed for a good harbor, while the city had easy access inland as well. That allowed it to trade both with the local Berber or Libyan population and with merchants across the sea. This foreign trade was what became the backbone of the Carthaginians' rise, as the city also had a favorable position in global trade. It stood on an important intersection of international trafficking routes linking the entire Mediterranean, both the east to the west and the north to the south. This shouldn't come as a surprise, though, as the New City was founded by the capable Phoenician merchants.

As such, Carthage quickly became an important factor in international trade, with archeological remains linking it with the Greeks in southern Italy and Greece, Egypt, Levant, and Spain. Its trading potential was only increased as the Phoenicians erected new cities, like, for example, in Sardinia, which only expanded the network, of which Carthage was a part of. The archeological evidence shows that it wasn't long before the New City reestablished its connections with Tyre, if they were ever even fully broken. Some historians even argue that Carthage's close ties with the Tyrian aristocracy, if there is any truth to Dido's myth, would only enhance its ties and place in the Phoenician trading system. However, the Carthaginians were not solely middlemen in these mercantile relations. It wasn't long before they began producing their own goods, most notably pottery, which was similar in style to the Greeks, and famous scarlet clothing dye from shellfish, for which the Phoenicians were already known. Archeologists also found evidence of iron foundries and other metallurgical shops from the earliest periods of the city, making metal products part of Carthage's exports as well.

Recent archeological discoveries additionally indicate that at some point, the Carthaginians developed the smelting technique of adding calcium to their furnaces, which neutralizes the sulfur in iron, improving its quality. As such, their ironmaking was likely very sought after in the Mediterranean world.

The rise of the New City's production and trade, as well as its favorable position, quickly attracted a new population. Newcomers came from various nations, who were openly welcomed by the Carthaginians. However, despite the urban globalism it attained, Carthage retained its Phoenician cultural heritage, which it held in high regard. Yet the influx of inhabitants meant that the city of Carthage grew rather quickly. According to researchers, in about a century, it had a population of roughly thirty thousand. They state that it took less than two centuries for it to grow to the size of its founding city, covering an area roughly 136 to 148 acres (55 to 60 hectares). In that period, which was no later than the early 7th century BCE, the city was enclosed by an almost ten-foot (three-meter) wide wall with bastions and gates. Yet despite that early growth, Carthage remained under the influence of Tyre, though likely with quite a broad autonomy. It would seem that despite the sharp break hinted in the myth of Dido, the reality was that Carthage remained a part of the Phoenician network. This is further proven by the founding of the new Phoenician colonies on Sardinia during the 7th century BCE. They were small settlements without any considerable public buildings, whose sole purpose seemed to be growing food for the Carthaginians and acquiring metal ores for its growing metallurgical industry.

Thus, by the end of the 7th century, it was clear that Carthage was a linchpin in the Phoenician trade network. The city quickly grew from a small provincial settlement into a bustling, fully developed urban center. However, it was not quite yet the Jewel of the West, prosperous, independent, and proud.

Chapter 2 – Becoming a Mediterranean Power

The early centuries of the Carthaginian history remain mostly blurry, faded by the long-gone centuries. In that period, the New City, despite its growth, remained just that, one of many Phoenician settlements in the west. We have very few details on its development, only broad outlines. However, this changed as historical circumstances pushed it into the light, allowing us to see its past much clearer from then on.

The rise of Carthage was caused by two significant changes in the political landscape of the Mediterranean world during the late 7th and early 6th centuries BCE. In the east, Tyre continued to spiral down in power and influence. It was pressured continuously by vast Mesopotamian empires, such as the Neo-Assyrians and Neo-Babylonians, who wanted to have such an important trading city under their control. Yet those empires were never fully capable of conquering the city itself. It was largely protected by its own importance both as a merchant power and an important source of precious metals, most notably silver. That led to an extended period, roughly from 800 to 600 BCE, during which Tyre was in a somewhat vassal relationship with whatever empire was in its hinterland. It paid tribute but was not under direct control. That was, in fact, the fate of most, if not all, Phoenician cities in the Levant at the time. However, in the late 7th century BCE, the value of silver began to collapse due to oversupply. The economic crisis of the Near East meant that the

14

mercantile influence of Tyre was dwindling, making it a much easier target for the Mesopotamians, as their empires were no longer dependent on it as a source of silver.

The added pressure on Tyre was enough for it to rebel in 586 against the Babylonians, who had supremacy over them at the time. Tyre was aided by the Egyptians, who were enemies of the Neo-Babylonian Empire, but it stood no real chance. For thirteen years, the city was besieged, but it did not fall. However, the city suffered economically as its trade was almost totally cut off. In the end, the city surrendered, accepting a humiliating peace, after which Tyre never recuperated completely. It was at this point that Carthage unquestionably gained its full independence, as its mother city was not able to influence it anymore. Yet even before this, Carthage was acting more or less on its own accord. During the latter part of the 7th century BCE, the Greeks began to expand more aggressively in Sicily and toward the Iberian Peninsula. As such, they began exerting pressure upon already existing Phoenician colonies. However, at the time, Tyre and other Phoenician cities were mostly too weak to help due to their problems with the Mesopotamians. This, in turn, pushed the Carthaginians to slowly rise as the leaders of all the Phoenician colonies in the west, as it was vital for them to protect the existing trade network upon which the New City relied for survival.

Despite that, the upsurge in Carthage's importance was not immediate. It was a slow process that took quite some time to evolve fully. In the last decades of the 7th and in the early 6th century, Carthage was acting more as an ally than a patron of the other Phoenician cities in the west. Circumstances changed in 580 BCE when the Sicilian Greeks tried to expel them from the entire island. Their motive for the attack was most likely caused by their wish to take control over trade with settlements in Sicily while further cutting off the Phoenicians from their colonies on Sardinia. The timing of the attack, coinciding with the siege of Tyre, also brings up the possibility that the Greeks were encouraged by the supposed weakness of the Phoenicians. However, there are no details regarding this in historical sources, which are sparse in general when talking about this attack. The ancient writers only mention that the attack failed, as the Phoenicians allied with the indigenous population from Sicily. The Carthaginians aren't referred to as direct participants in these early clashes. Still, after the Greek attack, they began intervening on the island. Keeping a foothold in Sicily became one of the Carthaginian cardinal policies, swaying their further development. Thus, it was the Greeks who prompted Carthage to become protectors and in the end rulers of the Phoenicians in the west.

Map of Phoenician and Greek colonization in mid-6th century.
Source: https://commons.wikimedia.org

Despite that, due to their ongoing conflicts with the Greeks and later the Romans, the ancient writers tended to categorize the Carthaginians as aggressive and imperialistic. That sentiment is, at the very least, historical propaganda, as the Carthaginians were no more hostile or hegemonic than the rest of the nations. Their activities were partly caused by the sympathy for their fellow Phoenicians, as well as their own trade interests. The idea of Carthage trying to occupy Phoenician colonies, especially in the 7th and 6th centuries, doesn't hold up when looking at the evidence. For example, Roman historian Justin claims that around that period, the Phoenician city of Gades or Gadir, modern-day Cadiz in southwest Spain, asked for Cartage's help against the indigenous population. They supposedly answered the plea but ended up acquiring Gades as a part of their empire. Archeological evidence disproves this story as there is no sign of occupation, and historians doubt it was even possible. At the time, the Carthaginians were still trying to gain influence over Sardinia and Sicily, and they were barely capable of achieving that. Thus, it was highly improbable they would be able to directly rule over a city more than 1,000 miles (1,600 kilometers) away. If Carthage did ever sent help, it was much later, and it didn't result in annexation.

On top of that, Justin claims that the Carthaginians were invited by the citizens of Gades, further tainting the possibility of Carthage's imperialism. However, this most likely made-up story hints at something else with this request. The Carthaginians were, in fact, maintaining close ties with their Phoenician brethren in Spain, keeping the trade alive. It kept a similar, if not closer, relationship with other Phoenician settlements across northwest Africa. Carthage's influence over those proliferated during the 5th century. Combined with forming new colonies on the African coast, the New City was slowly becoming a clear hegemon over that part of Africa, though its influence wasn't spread too deep inland. Their motivation for this was, as before, the necessity to keep their merchant network alive. Yet they were not content with only maintaining it. They sought to expand it as well. During the late 7th and early 6th centuries, Phoenicians, led by Carthage, began forming close trading ties with Etruscans, a nation that lived in modern-day Tuscany. It proved to be a rather fruitful relationship, as it was beneficial to both sides. Their bonds were further tightened when the Ionian Greeks, fleeing from the Persian conquest in the east, came to the northwestern Mediterranean around 540 BCE. The newcomers started pillaging the coasts, attacking both the Carthaginians and the Etruscans and disrupting their trade and colonies, which prompted the two nations to ally against them.

The main targets of the Greek pirates were the Etruscan colonies on Corsica and the Phoenician colonies on Sardinia, which were both rather weak and small. According to the written records, the outnumbered pirates were able to defeat the allied fleet but suffered such high casualties that they were forced to stop their plundering and retreat to the Greek colony of Massilia, also spelled as Massalia, modern-day Marseille in southern France. Thus, despite the defeat, the allies managed to deal with Greek piracy. From that point onward, relations between Etruscan cities, which were never united into a single state, and the Carthaginian towns flourished, and this friendship was crowned with official trading agreements in the late 6th century. At roughly the same time, the Carthaginians also approached a rising power in middle Italy, now known as the famous city of Rome. At the time, it was relatively young and still a fairly insignificant town, but the African merchants realized it had potential, and they began trading with it. The importance of this new business partner was recognized, and according to Roman histories in 509, in the first year of the Roman Republic, the two nations signed a friendship treaty. The exact year has since been debated by modern historians, with some claiming the recorded year is likely to be true. In contrast, others are more skeptical, dating it to a later period, somewhere between the late 5th or early 4th century.

The treaty between Carthage and Rome showcases two essential aspects of their relationship. Firstly, through the regulation of trade, it illuminates the fact that, at the time, the Phoenicians were much more powerful and influential. The treaty limited and ordered how the Romans had to trade on Phoenician soil, while the latter had no restrictions on how to conduct business in Roman territory. Secondly, it outlined the extent of Carthage's dominion in the Mediterranean, as it divided the spheres of influence between the two nations. Rome was confined to Italy, while Carthage was recognized as controlling Sicily, Sardinia, and northern Africa. It is important to note that even by the late 6th century, if we accept the traditional date, Spain isn't mentioned as part of Carthage's protectorate. That indicates that it was incorporated into what was to become its empire in a later period. The treaty also implies that Carthage was able to secure both its position in Sicily and Sardinia against the Greeks. Later Roman and

Greek historians claim that this consolidation of the Carthaginian power over the two islands happened in the second half of the 6th century, though their accounts are fragmented, conflicting, and at times vague. However, there is an outlining picture that could be roughly patched up from their works.

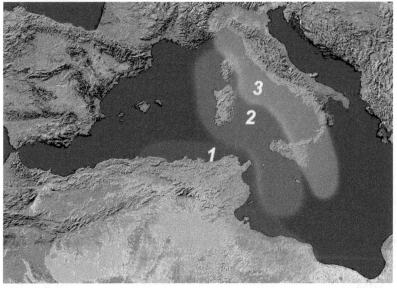

Division of Mediterranean according to the treaty of 509 - 1: Area prohibited to Rome, 2: Area tolerated in emergencies, 3: Open waters. Source: https://commons.wikimedia.org

Ancient historians tell us that a Carthaginian general named Malchus, whose Phoenician name was more likely Mazeus or Mazel, was sent to Sicily to secure Carthaginian positions. His historicalness is doubtful, causing much debate among historians, but if the sources are to be trusted, Malchus lived and led the Carthaginians between about 560 and 530 BCE. He commanded several expeditions on Sicily, in which he fought both the Greeks and quite likely some of the Phoenician cities opposing Carthage's influence or rule over them. These skirmishes or wars weren't constant but intermittent and with opponents often changing sides in them. Some of the sources claim he was ultimately unsuccessful, while others tell us he managed to fortify the Carthaginian grasp over the western part of the island. The truth is possibly somewhere in between, with Malchus being able to strengthen Carthaginian positions but not completely secure them. He is later attested as a leader of Carthage's troops in an alliance with the Etruscans. Despite gaining a strategic victory over the Greeks, it seems that Carthage's government saw his tactical defeat as a failure, sentencing him and his troops to exile. Some of the ancient writers convey that he and his soldiers rebelled afterward, possibly even attacking Carthage itself. In the end, it seems he was executed.

He was succeeded in the position of general by a man named Mago, who led the Carthaginian army both in Sicily and Sardinia. From the accounts, it seems he was more successful than his predecessor, possibly because the Carthaginian army was reformed at the time. It changed from the usual citizen levy to a mercenary army. This was done because Carthage had a population too small to sustain prolonged campaigns. Thus, it was seen as better for the citizens to continue their trading while the mercenary army would be paid from the taxes. In turn, Mago was later succeeded by his two sons, Hasdrubal and Hamilcar, though his exact fate is unknown. Familial ties and the fact that the Greek sources gave them titles of *basileus*, king in Greek, have led some historians to conclude that Mago may have usurped the power in Carthage. However, it seems that the Greeks mistakenly gave them the title as some ancient historians, for example, Herodotus, describes Hamilcar as a king because of his valor, not because it was his rightful title. Thus, modern historians think that Carthage remained a republic, whose structure and functions will be described in more detail in a later chapter. In that case, Mago and his Magonid house were not actual monarchs but only a political dynasty, which at the time held the highest offices in the state.

Despite not being true sovereigns, the Magonids were rather successful in defending Carthage and her interests. Around 515 BCE, the Greeks tried to settle near the Phoenician city of Lepcis, better known by its Roman name Leptis Magna, located in modern-day western Libya, at the mouth of the Wadi Lebdam in the Mediterranean. It was the easternmost city in Carthage's dominion. As such, the New City felt it was necessary to defend it against the Greeks, who were supposedly led by Spartan King Dorieous. With the help of the locals Libyans, they were defeated and chased away. Not long afterward, a border was established between Carthage's zone of influence and the Greek city of Cyrene, located in eastern Libya near present-day Shahhat. It was drawn around the modern town of Ra's Lanuf, on the coast of the Gulf of Sidra. Carthaginian influence in northern Africa was also spread to the west, to Gibraltar. On the seas, Carthage's dominion incorporated Phoenician colonies on the Balearic Islands, most notably on Ibiza. Under the leadership of the Magonids, the New City also continued to send small expeditions in an ongoing attempt to solidify control over both Sardinia and western Sicily.

That proved to be no easy task, as Hasdrubal lost his life fighting on Sardinia, most likely in 510. His younger brother Hamilcar, who became the new general, continued the fight. In that very same year, Dorieous once again tried to overstep the boundaries, settling this time in territories on Sicily, which Carthage saw as its sphere of influence. Carthage levied its army, either mercenary or from their local vassals, or even a mix of both, and by 509, the forces had forced the Spartan king out of their land. In the process, Dorieous and his followers lost their lives, putting an end to one of Carthage's problems. It is possible that some smaller expeditions were sent to Sardinia, as by that year, the already mentioned treaty with Rome states both islands as Carthage's undisputed dominion. It is important to note that this doesn't mean the indigenous population or the vassal Phoenicians never again rebelled. Smaller mutinies and revolts were possible, if not probable, but Carthage's influence was cemented henceforth. It also shows that both Mago's and Hasdrubal's contribution was significant, as Hamilcar only had to give finishing touches to it. The next roughly two decades were a peaceful period in Carthage's history, allowing for the newly attained territories to be better incorporated in the dominion.

Some historians tend to brand this as the beginning of Carthage's empire, which may be considered valid. The New City dominated much of the western Mediterranean, especially when it came to trading. However, it's important to note this empire was not structured as most others. Cities under Carthage's domination were still self-governed, with their local governments in place, but they paid their tributes and sent levies when asked. On the other hand, Carthage slowly became culturally dominant over its territories throughout the next couple of centuries. During this time, Carthage's subordinates gradually accepted the Carthaginian variation of the Phoenician language, its artistic styles and religious customs, and other aspects of its culture. It is also important to note that the Carthaginians also adopted some of the local traditions as well as foreign influences. Because of this, from the early 5th century BCE, we can talk about a Carthaginian civilization in its own right, not as a part of an old Phoenician one. Today, everything associated with it, from the language to the people, is often referred to as Punic, a Romanized variation of the Greek Phoenician. It is done so to differentiate it from its predecessor, though it should be noted that the Carthaginians never called themselves Punics (Punes) or their culture Punic.

Whether we accept that the Carthaginian sphere of influence was an empire, in its process of becoming one, or a "mere" dominion, one thing is clear. By the early 5th century, the New City managed to rise up, overcome countless hurdles, and become a leader of the western Mediterranean, which would eventually become known as the Punic world. However, its rise to power was not to end here, nor to remain unchallenged for too long.

Chapter 3 – Fighting for Control over Sicily

By the early 5th century, Carthage managed to become one of the most important actors on the historical stage. It was no longer just one of the many Phoenician cities in the west; it was the leader of the Punic world. This newly acquired status brought it more riches and power, but it also meant that it had to defend its positions against others aiming to take it. Thus, Carthage was ushered into the turbulent age of wars and conflicts.

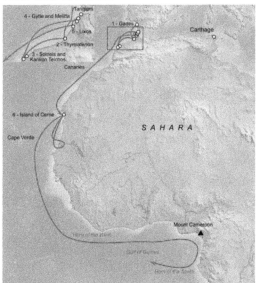

Possible route of Hanno's great voyage. Source: https://commons.wikimedia.org

However, before the significant conflicts with the Greeks began, there was a short period of peace and prosperity for the Carthaginians. It was in that period of the late 6th and early 5th centuries that Carthage was able to dispatch two exploratory expeditions in the Atlantic Ocean. Again, the primary sources for these are later Greek accounts, which means the exact year is unknown, prompting some historians to date it more toward the mid-5th century. However, it seems likely to assume these kinds of missions would be carried out during more peaceful times. The first voyage was led by Hanno, another high-ranking official in the republic, possibly also a member of the Magonids. He sailed with a large fleet, though the sources most likely exaggerate when mentioning 30,000 people, down the coast of Morocco and possibly farther south down the African coast. Due to vague descriptions and unfamiliar names of places and peoples mentioned in the account, modern historians are debating how far south the Carthaginians arrived. Some claim no farther than Senegal or Sierra Leone, while others state the Carthaginians went as far as Gabon or Cameroon, though the latter two seem less plausible. The goal of this expedition was twofold: one was to establish new colonies down the Atlantic coast and the other to explore new possible trading partners in the region.

The goals seem to have not been achieved. From the archeological evidence, it is clear that no long-lasting Punic settlement had been founded even on the southern Moroccan coast, while the texts don't mention any significant contacts with the locals to prompt any further trade. The longest-lasting impact of Hanno's voyage was, in fact, its account of capturing savage hairy humans that their local interpreters called "Gorillas." Later on, readers of this account assumed the Carthaginians had captured apes, prompting a 19th-century scientist to call a newly found species of apes by that name. At roughly the same time as Hanno's voyage, another Carthaginian, named Himilco, led a second expedition into the Atlantic. This group went the opposite way from Hanno, sailing up north instead. According to the later Roman sources, Himilco followed an already existing trade route used by the local Iberian population, at least to a certain point. Once again, the texts are vague, but most modern historians think that Himilco and his crew sailed all the way to the British Isles and northern France. It seems the goal of his voyage, unlike Hanno's, was only to establish trade connections. The success of the mission is questionable, but the archeological evidence suggests that Carthage's trade network at least reached the tin rich regions of modern-day Portugal.

Regardless of what the expeditions into the Atlantic achieved, the Carthaginians were keen on keeping the trade hegemony beyond Gibraltar for themselves. Some modern historians have even guessed that the vagueness, as well as the tales of sea monsters and other threats, were intentionally written to discourage others, mainly Greeks, from trying to venture that far west. This is possible, as despite having a formidable navy, the Carthaginians were not able to control or block the seas entirely. None of the ancient naval powers were able to do that due to the technological limitations of the era. On the other hand, the Greeks continued to try to thaw the Carthaginian wariness, especially on Sicily. In the early 6th century, the Greek cities on the island were going through political upheavals, with the Ionian and the Dorian Greeks starting to clash. This was only furthered by the rise of the tyrants in cities who simply sought more power for themselves. One of the Dorian tyrants named Gelo, whose capital was at one point the famous Sicilian city of Syracuse, dreamt of uniting the entire island under his rule. Allied with another Dorian despot called Theron, he actively waged wars against the Ionians during the 480s. Their opponents, the Ionians, realized that on their own, they were helpless; thus, in 483 BCE, they turned to Carthage for help.

The New City was aware that it had to intervene. If the Dorians were to unite all of the Greek territories in Sicily, the Carthaginian cities in the western regions of the island would be seriously threatened. However, for unknown reasons, their help was held back for three whole years before Hamilcar was sent with the largest expeditionary force amassed by the Carthaginians at that time. Ancient historians claim it was no less than 300,000 strong, but modern assessments usually don't go much higher than 30,000. Most of these, if not all, were mercenaries who were transported by the Carthaginian fleet. It supposedly consisted of 3,000 transport and 200 battleships. The latter number is in the range of reality, as it represents the Punic potential, but it is also likely to have been far smaller, while the number of transports is surely significantly exaggerated. Gelo's force wasn't much smaller; according to the sources, he had around 26,000 soldiers. In that regard, the two sides were quite evenly matched, but Gelo proved to be more opportunistic and cunning. Near the city of Himera, in northern Sicily, he intercepted a message Hamilcar sent to his Sicilian allies, in which Hamilcar expected them to send cavalry as reinforcements. Gelo saw an opportunity and sent his own cavalry instead to meet with the Carthaginians near their anchored ships. The rouse was successful; the Syracusans burnt most of the vessels, killed Hamilcar, and then turned toward the main Carthaginian camp, completely destroying the mercenary force.

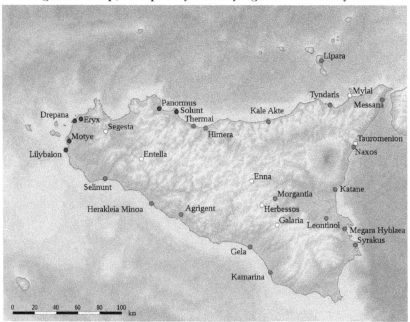

Map of colonies on Sicily (purple marks Carthaginian and red Greek cities).
Source: https://commons.wikimedia.org

The Greek victory was absolute, but Gelo was wise enough to realize that the Carthaginians were still strong enough to defend their own cities in Sicily. Thus, he sued for peace, asking only for two thousand talents (about fifty tons of silver), and the Punes had to build two temples where the treaty would be displayed. Carthage was eager to accept. Ancient Greek historians later hinted that this Carthaginian "attack," as they saw it, was arranged with the Persian Empire, as in that very same year, Xerxes I launched his attack on the Greeks. Modern historians, on the other hand, highly doubt it. The Persians certainly knew enough about Carthage as the new masters of Tyre. They even supposedly wanted to conquer it around 525 BCE, but their attempt was thwarted by the refusal of the Phoenicians to fight their brethren. However, there is no other evidence than timing itself to connect the two wars. On the other hand, until recently, modern historians have often overexaggerated the scope of the Carthaginian defeat, attributing it as the reason for bleak times through which the Punic state went through afterward. Still, the losses at the Battle of Himera were insufficient to singlehandedly cause the contraction of Carthage's power. Most of the troops lost were mercenaries, while the fact that Gelo decided not to pursue further battles meant that Carthage had either more ships or capabilities to recover their losses quickly.

Nonetheless, in the decades after 480 BCE, Carthage went through sort of a recession. After their victories over the Persians, the Greek power continued to rise, and they managed to become masters of the eastern Mediterranean, with Athens leading the Greek hegemony. This meant that for the Carthaginians, their traditional markets in Phoenicia and Egypt were closed for them. At roughly the same time, Rome began pressuring the Etruscans, old Punic allies. This meant that Carthage lost another important trading partner. This isolation, more than the defeat at Himera, caused the slowing down of Carthaginian expansion. Yet, despite that, during that period, Carthage wasn't idle. Her focus merely changed due to the circumstances. Now the New City decided to expand its territories in

North Africa. It began spreading more inland, incorporating the local population into its state, which proved to be a difficult task. The Berbers were trailing behind the Carthaginians in civilizational development, and more importantly, their culture was significantly different. Thus, even though the Punes weren't enslaving the Berbers en masse or tried to forcibly remove them from their lands, the local African population never fully merged with the Carthaginians. The Carthaginians did treat them differently from their own population, placing higher taxes and imposing levies on them. Furthermore, it seems they tried to impose their own culture on the Berbers, which was mostly unsuccessful.

The attempts to integrate the local population marks the beginning of Carthage's transformation from a dominion toward more of an empire. It was in this time that the New City began imposing its own administration upon its subordinate towns and settlements. Coupled with that was the political reform in the city itself. New democratic offices and political institutions were supposedly created to limit the power and influence of the aristocratic families, most notably the Magonids. However, despite the democratic feel of these reforms, Carthage remained an oligarchy republic with the Magonids at its head. This prompted some modern historians to conclude that the Magonids themselves were a part of the reforms. It's possible they tailored them to their own political needs at the time, maybe to relieve some pressure on the family after the defeat at Himera. In any case, Hamilcar seems to have been succeeded by his son Hanno. There isn't much evidence about him, but due to his name, some historians have linked him to be the famous explorer who sailed down to Africa. This is questionable but possible. If that is the case, the expeditions happened fifty years later, around 450 BCE, and it meant that the Magonids and Carthage recovered quicker than expected. This theory also explains that the voyages had been undertaken in an attempt to break the Punic isolation of the 5th century. However, it should be noted that both theories are based more on conjecture than on evidence. So far, no conclusive proof has been found for either of them.

A 19ᵗʰ-century artistic representation of the Battle of Himera (480 BCE).
Source: https://commons.wikimedia.org

Regardless of the exact dates of the expeditions, it seems that modern historians have slightly overexaggerated the extent of the Carthaginian crisis. Due to the expansion in Africa, the New City was less reliant on imported foodstuffs. New territories became its chief supplier, along with more developed Sardinian colonies. The trading ties with the Iberian Phoenician colonies expanded, bringing them closer under the influence of the Punic world. Finally, the lack of any major wars and conflicts meant that the Carthaginian treasury was growing richer. It was enough to impress the Greeks, most notably the wealthy Athenians, as Carthage reappears once again in the spotlight of the Greek writers. On top of that, the Athenians were also impressed by the military power of the Punes, with one of their generals claiming it was stronger than Athens. This accumulation of wealth and military might was due to decades of avoiding conflicts with the Greeks and the indigenous population of Sicily. It's not clear why, but it seems that for roughly seventy years, Carthage was content with her position on the island, while other states didn't encroach on her territory. For that reason, the New City remained out of the focus of the Greek writers, possibly enhancing our visage on the supposed crisis through which Carthage had been going through in the 5th century BCE.

Yet as the century neared its end, Carthage became a more prominent actor in the Greek world. The Athenians, capable traders themselves, realized the potential of partnering with the Carthaginians. Thus, relations between the two thalassocracies began to develop. In 416, Athens sent an expedition to Sicily to fight against Syracuse. It was an ambitious attempt to gain the upper hand in the Peloponnesian War against Sparta, in which Syracuse was on the side of the Spartans. According to some ancient historians, Athens also planned to conquer Carthage, which seems improbable. In contrast, others mention it asking for the help of the Punes. Wisely, the Carthaginians chose to once again stay out of the fight, leaving the two other Mediterranean forces to weaken themselves. By 413 BCE, Syracuse won with the help of the Spartans. This increased its power and dominance over the island as it began to seek revenge on the Sicilian cities that had sided with the Athenians. One of them, Segesta, in 410, asked for Carthaginian protection in exchange for its submission to the Punic dominion. After seventy years of passiveness in Sicily, Carthage decided to accept the offer and step in.

Several reasons prompted the Carthaginians, who were under the leadership of Hannibal Mago, the grandson of Hamilcar, to intervene this time. Most importantly, Syracuse's power was growing quickly, and its appetites rose with it. Secondly, the position of Segesta, on the northwestern tip of Sicily, was too close to the Punic territories. If it fell into Syracusan hands, Carthage's hold on the western parts of the island would be threatened. On the other hand, by that time, the strength of the Punic state had grown due to its expansion in northern Africa. Carthage needed a new direction to expand, with Sicily being the logical choice. Also, it is not unimportant to note that the Athenians completely lost their interests in Sicily, which gave

Carthaginians carte blanche to do as they pleased on the island. This was further proved when the two sea powers signed a treaty of friendship in 406 BCE. Some of the Greek historians also mention that Hannibal set out to avenge his grandfather, but this seems more than unlikely. If he was driven by passion, he would have done it far sooner. It is more likely that this reasoning was formed due to the Greeks once again overplaying the importance of the Battle of Himera in history.

The war that ensued was fought with previously unseen ferocity. In 409, the Carthaginian expedition once again mainly consisted of the mercenary soldiers and the Carthaginian navy. Hannibal led them to two great victories over the cities of Selinus and Himera, which were both sacked and razed before the Carthaginians triumphantly returned to Africa. Despite losing their allies, Syracuse remained inactive during this campaign. However, one of its renegade generals raided Punic territories afterward. This prompted Hannibal Mago to return in 406 BCE with even more fury. He laid siege to the city of Akragas, modern Agrigento in southern Sicily, which was the most crucial Syracusan ally and one of the wealthiest Greek settlements on the island. During this battle, the plague ravaged the Carthaginian army, taking Hannibal with it. Still, his cousin and successor, Himilco II, managed to conquer and pillage the city. He then proceeded with capturing and sacking the cities of Gela and Camarina, slowly advancing toward Syracuse itself. On his way, he managed to defeat the Syracusan army, which was under the leadership of its new tyrant, Dionysius I. Despite these victories, the Carthaginians were still burdened by the plague, which led Himilco to agree to a peace treaty before landing a final blow to Syracuse.

It was agreed that the southern Greek cities from Akragas to Camarina would pay tribute to Carthage, and the independence of other towns in Sicily's center and northeast would be guaranteed, while the Punic dominion in the western parts of the island would be recognized. It was a favorable peace for the Carthaginians, leaving Syracuse isolated, at least on paper. However, the Carthaginians brought the plague back home, causing its government to focus on internal matters. This allowed Dionysius to ignore the treaty and conquer many of the eastern and central Sicilian cities. By around 398 BCE, Syracuse managed to rebuild its strength, gathering reportedly 80,000 soldiers, a probable exaggeration, and 200 ships. Figuring that the Punes were devastated by the illness, he besieged the island city of Motya, one of the most important Carthaginian cities on the western coast of Sicily. With large siege towers, the Syracusans were able to breach the walls, proceeding to fight on the roofs, which were connected with wooden planks. The city was ravaged and never recovered. The Carthaginians were furious. Himilco gathered the troops and returned to the island during the winter, a season during which, in ancient times, armies rarely fought. He forced out the small Syracusan force that was left in Motya and retook it. Nevertheless, Himilco chose not to rebuild the ruined city but decided to build a new one just south of it, which we know by the Latinized name Lilybaeum.

Modern reconstruction of the island city of Motya. Source: https://commons.wikimedia.org

The victory at Motya wasn't enough to appease the Carthaginians, and Himilco sailed to the northeastern tip of Sicily, capturing and pillaging the city of Messana. His troops then marched south, toward Syracuse, while the navy followed down the coast. Dionysius tried to stop the Carthaginian fleet but was defeated in the Battle of Catana in

397 BCE. By the winter of that year, Syracuse was besieged, as its defenses were too strong for the Carthaginians to attack. At that point, it seemed as if the Punic victory was at hand, as Himilco hoped the Syracusans would depose their tyrant and ask for peace. However, fortune once again turned against the Carthaginians. As the summer of 396 approached, another epidemic ravaged the Punic army, severely weakening it. Dionysius exploited this and began attacking the Carthaginian camps and navy. Himilco found himself in a position to be cut off, prompting him to retreat with his Carthaginian soldiers on the ships and escape to Africa, leaving the mercenaries and Sicilian allies on their own. Later, many Greek sources mention that he bribed Dionysius to escape, but it seems unlikely that even a greedy tyrant would choose short-term gain over a total victory. Nonetheless, Himilco's cowardly move was met with massive dissatisfaction in Carthage, as he was judged for leaving the rest of the army on its own.

Himilco accepted full blame for the defeat, and the disgrace soon drove him to suicide. More worryingly for Carthage, it seems that his abandonment of non-Carthaginian troops prompted the local Libyans to rebel, as they made up part of those forces. This was accompanied by a slave uprising as well, singling that there was much dissatisfaction in the Punic empire in Africa. During that turmoil, a man named Mago, Himilco's deputy, was chosen to be the highest official. Most historians assume he was a part of the Magonid family, possibly Himilco's nephew. However, some scholars are doubtful of that, as they claim there is no clear evidence to support that fact. Regardless of his familial ties, Mago managed to quell the uprisings before returning to Sicily. He clashed several times with the Syracusans, with mixed results. By 392 BCE, both sides were tired of the prolonged war and agreed to a peace treaty. It was similar to the previous agreement, with both sides keeping their spheres of influence, except for central Sicily, which Carthage left to Dionysius. Yet the peace was merely an interim, as no conclusive victory was gained. Dionysius began to expand the Syracusan dominion, acquiring territories in eastern Sicily and even in southern Italy. In the meantime, Carthage continued to prepare for the war it foresaw.

In 383 BCE, Dionysius crossed the line when he sought alliances with some of the cities in western Sicily, which were a part of the Carthaginian sphere of influence. The Punes immediately went to war, sending Mago to deal with him once again. The exact chronology and details of this new conflict are rather sketchy. It seems that Mago sent a detachment to southern Italy, where, allied with the Italics, they pressured Syracuse on a second front. Mago himself led the campaign in Sicily, where he suffered a crushing defeat, losing his life in the process. Carthage was ready for peace, but Dionysius gave an impossible ultimatum: The Punes had to abandon Sicily. In response, the New City instated Mago's son, presumably named Himilco, as its new general. He managed to defeat the Syracusans in a battle near modern-day Palermo around 376 BCE, prompting Dionysius to accept peace. Syracuse had to pay one thousand talents, and a demarcation line between the two powers was drawn. It went along the river Halycus, today's Platani, just west of Akragas, while in the north, Carthage gained the territory of Thermae Himeraeae, a successor city of Himera. Besides gaining considerable territory on the island, the Punes were also eager to end this conflict as soon as possible. However, the plague once again ravaged the city of Carthage, while the Libyans and Sardinians revolted at the same time.

Afterward, Himilco disappears from the sources. If he was indeed part of the Magonid family, with him, its dominance waned as they also vanished from the forefront of Carthaginian politics. By the late 370s, a man named Hanno, sometimes nicknamed as "the Great," appeared on the stage, quelling the rebellions. Unlike the Magonids in previous decades, he was opposed by Suniatus, which is a Latinized form of the Punic name Eshmuniaton. Thus, Punic politics entered a more fluid state. At the same time, Dionysius saw another opportunity to attack the supposedly weak Carthage, as it was still recuperating from the plague and uprisings. In 368, he attempted to conquer Lilybaeum, but Hanno was able to destroy the Syracusan fleet and force the aging tyrant to retreat. Dionysius I soon died, and his son and namesake, Dionysius II, accepted the peace in which the status quo was arranged. A decade of peace ensued, but it was broken when Syracuse plunged into a state of civil war. Dionysius II was ousted, and other Greek cities plunged into anarchy, with petty tyrants fighting for power. Despite that, Carthage itself stayed aloof. Hanno was too consumed with Carthaginian politics to pursue any gains in Sicily.

First off, he had to depose his main adversary. Hanno accused Suniatus of traitorous contacts with Dionysius, and by most likely using strong anti-Syracusan sentiment in the city, Hanno had him executed. Yet Hanno wasn't satisfied; despite losing their leader, opposition in Carthage was still very much alive. It seems that Hanno's arrogance and ambition lost him the support of most of the citizens. Aware of that, but still hungry for more power, around 350 BCE, Hanno planned a coup. First, he tried to murder a number of high-ranking state officials at his daughter's wedding banquet. The plot was discovered and avoided, prompting Hanno to retreat to his country estate for a last stand. Sources mention he tried to organize a slave revolt, though this is doubtful. He likely assembled his followers and some slaves on his estate while trying fruitlessly to win the support of the Libyans. Hanno was captured, mutilated, and finally crucified for his treachery, while his family seemed to be exiled, even though some sources mention them being executed as well. The opposition, without any particular leader that we know of, then turned its gaze upon Sicily once again.

By 345 BCE, Syracuse was under the control of Hicetas, who had strong ties to Carthage. He asked for help from the Punes when the old tyrant Dionysius II attempted to retake the city. Since the newly established leaders of Carthage needed military successes to solidify their rule, they were eager to help. A massive Carthaginian army was sent to Sicily, entering Syracuse in 344. However, at the same time, a smaller contingent of Greek troops from the city of Corinth, located in mainland Greece arrived, as Hicetas asked Corinth for assistance as well. This led to a somewhat confusing four-way standoff, as all sides attempted to fulfill their plans. In the end, the Corinthians, who were led by Timoleon, were the most successful. Timoleon exiled Dionysius to Corinth, Hicetas escaped, and by 343, the Carthaginians withdrew without a fight. This undecisive Punic action was met with substantial public outrage, as they had been in the city itself, prompting the leading Carthaginian general to take his own life. Timoleon proceeded to raid the Carthaginian territory, as he required resources to pay his troops, while moving to strengthen his positions in Sicily. The Punic response was rather slow, as it wasn't until 341 that a new expeditionary force was sent to the island. This time, alongside with usual mercenaries, a so-called Sacred Battalion, consisting of about three thousand elite aristocratic Carthaginians as well as another seven thousand regular citizens, were sent.

An artistic representation of a battle between the Carthaginians and the Greeks.
Source: https://commons.wikimedia.org

Despite having a numerical advantage, the Punic army was defeated by Timoleon in the Battle of the Crimissus, mostly thanks to terrible commanders. As a result, the Sacred Battalion and other Carthaginian citizens were killed or enslaved. The defeat was total, and the New City was panicking. They recalled Hanno's son Gisco from exile, giving him full control to prepare for the Greek invasion.

Instead, Gisco managed to forge a peace with Timoleon, who had his hands full with the petty Greek tyrants in Sicily. The result of this disastrous war for Carthage was more than acceptable, though, given they went back to the *status quo* positions of 367 while promising to cut all ties with the petty Greek tyrants.

For a couple of decades, the Punes left Sicily on its own. First of all, the city needed to recover from its losses while also bringing some balance to its politics. The need for this was only furthered when Alexander the Great began his conquest of Persia in 334 BCE. Within two years, he managed to conquer Tyre from the Persians, and the Carthaginians accepted refugees from their mother city, mostly children and women. Next in line was Egypt, an old trading partner of Carthage. The Punes were afraid they could be next in line as they possessed a rich land, and Alexander reportedly warned them he would attack once he was finished with Persia. That left the Carthaginians to prepare for a possible invasion.

However, Alexander's premature death in 323 eased their fears, once again opening a possibility to meddle in Sicilian affairs. By that time, a general named Hamilcar, possibly with familial ties to Gisco, took over the rudder of the republic. It seems he attempted to retain peace and good relations with Syracuse, interfering in its internal affairs after Timoleon's death. At first, the Carthaginians supported the oligarchs before switching their backing to a populist tyrant named Agathocles. Hamilcar even led a military intervention in 319 to secure Agathocles's position. He hoped that a personal agreement with an established ruler of Syracuse would make peace last longer, but he was wrong. Agathocles first removed any opposition in the city, then attempted to conquer Messana in 315. Hamilcar's envoys stopped Agathocles from that and, in the very next year, managed to put off a boiling conflict between Syracuse and its Sicilian opponents. The preserved peace was short-lived, though. The Syracusans soon seized Messana, and in 312 BCE, they attacked Akragas, where the Punic fleet stopped them. In retaliation, Agathocles invaded and plundered the Carthaginian territories in western Sicily. The failure of Hamilcar's policy was evident. Thus, he was supposedly convicted in his absence, but Hamilcar died before he could return to Carthage. His replacement was Gisco's son, confusingly also named Hamilcar.

The new general proved to be much more capable. He forged alliances with many Greek towns that opposed Agathocles and defeated him at the battle of Gela in 311. The combined Greco-Punic army then proceeded to besiege Syracuse. Instead of attempting to passively defend the city, Agathocles acted with unprecedented audacity. In the summer of 310, he slipped through the naval blockade and attacked the Carthaginians in Africa. What ensued was a period of total chaos. An unexpected attack on its hinterland caught Carthage by surprise. The Syracusans were able to conquer several important cities, including Utica and Tunes (modern-day Tunis), and defeated the Punic army on several occasions. In one of the battles, a new Sacred Battalion was lost, as well as Hanno, one of the two Carthaginian generals tasked with overseeing the fighting in Africa. The Carthaginian positions only deteriorated when the Libyan revolts began to ravage across its African empire. By 309, Hamilcar was defeated in Sicily, losing his life in the process. The Greek allies then abandoned the Carthaginian leadership and began to fight on their own, even amongst each other. The situation was so desperate for Carthage that its other African general, Bomilcar, attempted a coup in 308 BCE. He wanted to become a Carthaginian tyrant whose rule would be unrestrained by the republican institutions.

Despite the chaos of the Punic state, the Carthaginians were unwilling to succumb to despotic rule. The citizens stood against Bomilcar, who obviously lacked any broader support, capturing and executing him before he could finalize his coup. It is around that time that the war turned against Agathocles, as Syracuse came under pressure from other Greek cities on Sicily. The tyrant was forced to return to the island, yet he left his troops under the command of his son in Africa. Those forces continued to plunder, but the Carthaginians were able to contain them without the leadership of Agathocles. These men were encircled in Tunes by the Punic army, prompting Agathocles to return in 307. Yet he was defeated upon his arrival. Realizing his African adventure was over, the tyrant escaped, leaving his trapped troops with two of his sons to be captured and killed. By that time, both Syracuse and Carthage had enough of war. Carthage was still facing Berber rebellions, while Syracuse was facing its Greek foes in Sicily. By 306, the war was over. The boundary between the Syracusan and Carthaginian zones of influence was once again settled at the Halycus River, while the Punes also paid a smaller subsidy for the liberation of their nominally occupied territories.

The war, which Carthage had tried to avoid, proved to be the most devastating for the republic. The losses were high, and the gains almost nonexistent. Yet the Carthaginians were forced to fight it, if nothing else than to preserve their territories and position in Sicily. In fact, the result of the Sicilian Wars, as this series of conflicts fought between Syracuse and Carthage was later named by historians, could be summed up similarly. The Punes fought for nearly 180 years to retain their grip on the western portion of the island, but they never gained much for their ventures. In the end, they at least managed to withstand the pressure from the Greeks. Yet their biggest foes were still to challenge them.

Chapter 4 – From Allies to Enemies

While Carthage was preoccupied with its dealings with the Greeks in Sicily, another power rose to prominence in its neighborhood. Rome, once a small city in central Italy, managed through the years to conquer not only Latium but also the Etruscans and other surrounding nations and tribes. At first, the Punes had no quarrel with them as they were seen as lucrative trading partners.

The Carthaginian pragmatic merchant attitude toward the Romans was evident since their first trade agreement of 509. The Etruscans, old Punic allies, were already fighting with the rising power of the Roman state. Yet the Carthaginians stood aside, looking only to trade and profit. Roughly 160 years later, in 348 BCE, a new treaty was signed between Rome and Carthage. Like the previous one, it was a set of rules in mutual dealings between the two republics. For example, it stated that if Roman or Carthaginian merchants had to stop to resupply in the other state's territory, they shouldn't harm the locals and must leave within five days. The Romans were allowed free trade with the Carthaginians in Sicily, while they were banned from trading in Sardinia, Spain, and Africa. On the other hand, the Punes were free to trade in Roman lands. It went beyond trade as well, as it also barred the Romans from plundering and founding colonies in those territories. Similarly, Carthage was forbidden from conquering any cities in Latium. Furthermore, it was agreed that if, for example, a

Roman envoy brought captives from a nation with whom Carthage had an official treaty to a Punic city, the Carthaginians had the right to liberate them. This also applied to the Carthaginians.

However, this treaty raises several questions. Firstly, despite banning the Romans from founding cities in Africa and Sardinia, Carthage stayed silent about Sicily. Similarly, the Punes weren't forbidden from founding colonies in Latium. Yet it is clear that for both sides, such actions would be out of the question. Secondly, by the mid-4th century, Rome was much stronger and more influential than in 509. Nonetheless, the second treaty imposes further bans on Roman trading rights in the western Mediterranean. It is peculiar that a much stronger Rome would accept such harsher terms. The reasoning behind it could be different needs from the treaty. Carthage was attempting to recuperate economically from the financial losses of the rebellions in the 370s. Furthermore, it was, in general, a trading-oriented state, prompting it to focus more on the economic aspects of the agreement. On the other hand, Rome was militaristic and expansionistic, caring less about trading. Its primary concern would be to ban Carthage from meddling in its neighboring regions, allowing Rome to enlarge its own territory. Whatever may be the exact reasoning behind both sides accepting such an agreement, it could be said that it was a diplomatic achievement for the Punes. They managed to secure their positions against Rome despite the fact they were going through rather turbulent times.

The third treaty between Rome and Carthage, which was signed in 306 BCE, is the most controversial one. There is no factual proof of it other than reports of some Roman historians several decades later. Even then, it was a matter of debate among Roman scholars if it was real or made up. It was especially important to them as it supposedly banned Romans from entering Sicily and Carthaginians from entering Italy. If the treaty was genuine, the late Punic Wars would be blamed on the Romans. Thus, many Romans have disregarded it. However, modern historians tend to believe this agreement existed, as it fits the international politics at the time. The Romans had gained hegemony over most of Italy, except the southern Greek colonies. It was likely their hope to conquer those as well, thus prompting them to seek a way to limit possible Punic interference. On the other hand, the Carthaginians were exhausted by their last war with Syracuse. Securing peace in Sicily against possible Roman expansion on the island surely seemed like another diplomatic victory. Simultaneously, because of the Sicilian Wars, Carthage was in no shape to actually consider meddling in Italian affairs. Similarly, the Romans at the end of the 4th century were busy with their wars with the Samnites and what was left of the Etruscans to plan any expeditions to Sicily. From the perspectives of both republics, this treaty would have been a deal without any downsides.

A 19ª-century illustration of Carthaginian merchants (left) trading with a Roman.
Source: https://commons.wikimedia.org

After 306, Carthage enjoyed a brief period of peace. It lasted until Agathocles's death in 289 when Greek cities in Sicily once again reverted to their chaotic politics. Petty tyrants rose up, while Agathocles's Campanian mercenaries, known as the Mamertines, began ravaging the island, even seizing Messana for themselves in the process. In Syracuse, a new tyrant named Hicetas arose, and it wasn't long before he raided the Carthaginian territories. He was likely hoping for easy plunder and a victory to reinforce his position as a tyrant. Instead, in 280 BCE, he was defeated by the Punes and later overthrown by his rivals. However, this was enough for the Carthaginians to be vengeful. They gathered troops and ships and once again besieged Syracuse, which was also involved in internal strife amongst its leaders. It was at this point that the Greeks, presumably the Syracusans, asked Pyrrhus, the king of Epirus, to help them against the Carthaginians. At the time, Pyrrhus was warring against the Romans in Italy, as he had been invited by the Greek cities there to help them against the Latin expansion. He commanded a sizeable army and had shown prowess as a general. Yet he was unable to defeat the Romans, leading to a stalemate in Italy.

Pyrrhus was an adventurer thirsty for glory and conquest, so when he received a call for help from the Syracusans to fend off "the barbarians" attacking fellow Greeks, he didn't think too much about it, especially as it meant breaking off the deadlocked conflict with the Romans. However, the Carthaginians caught wind of this and negotiated another treaty with the Latins in 279. It confirmed the previous agreements but also added a non-compulsory alliance against Pyrrhus. In essence, no side was obliged to help, but it left the possibility of Carthage aiding the Romans with their navy, while the Romans would contribute land troops if need be. Despite the vague alliance between the two republics, neither side ended up requesting or offering assistance. In 278 BCE, Pyrrhus finally arrived on Sicily and initiated a lightning-fast campaign. First, he liberated Syracuse, where the Carthaginians retreated at the sight of his army. Then, aided by Sicilian allies, he proceeded to conquer several Punic cities in Sicily before laying siege to the heavily-fortified town of Lilybaeum. Taken by surprise with the speed and force of the Greeks, the Carthaginians tried to negotiate with Pyrrhus. They offered him money and ships to transport his troops back to Italy, but he declined. He was supposedly preparing to invade Africa and conquer Carthage itself.

It is unclear if these ambitions were real, but they align with his adventurous personality. However, his Sicilian allies were against such ventures. They began suspecting that Pyrrhus started dreaming of creating his own empire in the west. His position worsened as his allies began defecting due to his harsh treatment. By 276, the king of Epirus received another plea for help from the Italian Greeks, giving him yet another excuse to leave a stalemate of his creation. After he left, the Carthaginians had little trouble in retaking all their lost cities, while the Syracusans became more concerned with the raiding Mamertines. Thus, the peace was renewed with the territorial status quo. The only marginal gain of the Carthaginians was the fact that Syracuse lost its grip on some of the Greek cities in Sicily, like Akragas, which established friendlier relations with the Punes. Up north, in Italy, Pyrrhus was defeated by the Romans. He fled back to Epirus, while the Latins continued their conquest. By 270 BCE, the Latins controlled most of Italy. Despite their supposedly friendly or even allied relations, the Carthaginians became somewhat wary of the Roman expansion.

However, after achieving peace in Sicily, the Carthaginians remained as composed as before. They attempted to retain the peace and balance of power both with Syracuse and Rome. Yet after a few years, a new Syracusan ruler named Hiero decided to end Mamertine rule over Messana, besieging them in 264 BCE. Trapped, the Campanian mercenaries called both the Romans and the Punes for assistance. The Carthaginians were the first to arrive, yet after learning that Rome decided to answer their call as well, the Campanian mercenaries sent them away. It seems that due to their Italian background, they felt closer to the Latins. This caused considerable turmoil among the Carthaginians. The commander of the Punic forces sent to Messana was even crucified, supposedly for his stupidity. More importantly, it appears that the Carthaginian fears had begun to materialize, as Rome started to expand into Sicily. Almost immediately, the Punes sent a new army to the island, while their diplomats began gathering allies. In a surprising turn of events, the

Carthaginians found them in Akragas and, even more unexpectedly, in Syracuse. Now allies, the two most powerful forces of Sicily laid siege to Messana. Seeing a new unified Sicilian force, the Romans had second thoughts about meddling in the island's affairs. One of the Roman consuls sent a negotiation offer, but both the Carthaginians and the Syracusans declined, effectively starting a conflict that was to become known as the First Punic War.

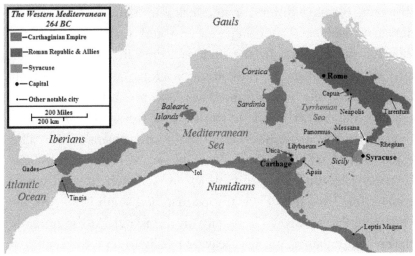

Approximate borders prior to the First Punic War. Source: https://commons.wikimedia.org

Ever since the 3ʳᵈ century BCE, there has been a debate about who was to blame for the beginning of this conflict. Even the Roman historians themselves debated the issue. If the treaties from 306 and 279 existed, and most modern historians argue they did, then the Roman decision to interfere and send troops to the Mamertines would have been a breach of an agreement. From the Carthaginian side, it is clear that a Roman presence in Sicily would be a threat, a sign of Latin expansionism on the island. Others have debated that Rome was fearful of Carthage attempting to expand its sphere of influence in southern Italy, in regions once closely tied to Syracuse. However, the initial reactions show that the Latins weren't expecting to fight the Punes, especially when considering the fact that they offered to negotiate as soon as they realized the Carthaginians were against them. It looks like the Roman plan was to fight against the growing power of Syracuse, which could have potentially threatened Roman gains in Italy. It is not unimaginable that the Romans thought that warring against the Carthaginians' traditional enemy wouldn't cause any troubles with their nominal allies. It is also worth mentioning that there weren't any signs of the Carthaginians attempting to expand into Italy, as it always seemed too far out of their reach.

However, blaming Rome for interfering in Sicily or Carthage for acting aggressively and refusing peace would only mask the real reasons for the conflict. In the end, it seems that the war started because of miscalculations, miscommunications, and, most notably, fears. And once the war began, there was no turning back. The Roman forces crossed over to Sicily with about 16,000 troops, defeating first the Syracusans then the Carthaginians. Both allies retreated to their territories, effectively ceasing to act in unison. This was exploited by the Latin army, which immediately pressed toward its primary foe, Syracuse. Their troops marched south from Messana and besieged the strongest Greek city on the island. At the time, the Carthaginians remained inactive, leaving its ally to fend for itself. It is unclear why the Punes acted so lethargic against the Romans. Some scholars have suggested that based on their previous experience, the Carthaginians predicted Syracuse would able to hold on for a long time, even under siege. With such calculations, it might have seemed to the Carthaginians that they had enough time to gather troops and adequately prepare for war. However, they were wrong. When Hiero saw that the Carthaginians weren't coming to help, he arranged peace with the Romans. By the summer of 263 BCE, Carthage lost its ally.

Syracuse was allowed to keep some of its possessions in eastern Sicily but had to pay a modest sum of one hundred talents, roughly the yearly pay for five thousand Roman legionnaires. Most importantly for the Romans, Hiero also obliged to provide supplies for the Latin forces on the island. Thus, Syracuse became a Roman ally. After this victory, half of the Roman army was sent back to Italy, showing once again that at that point, Rome was still unsure how to proceed in this unexpected war with Carthage. However, the other half of the army, led by a Roman consul, marched toward the Punic territories. There, they avoided any significant confrontations or sieges, but they managed to persuade several Carthaginian cities to defect. The most important of them was Segesta. Throughout the rest of the year, the Carthaginians remained inactive, as they lacked an army large enough to take on the remaining Roman troops. Thus, they opted for passive defense concentrated at significant fortified points. This tactic had worked for them in the past against the Greeks, but it wasn't enough to deter the Romans. A change was needed if Carthage hoped to stop defections of its allies and dependencies; thus, in 262, a large mercenary army was gathered and sent to Sicily.

The reinforcements arrived at Akragas, the largest Greek ally Carthage had, yet the Punes remained passive. However, it is unclear if that was by choice. A new Roman army, which had arrived on Sicily at almost the same time, besieged the city rather promptly, stopping any possible offensive planned by the Carthaginian general named Hannibal. Soon, another Carthaginian army, led by yet another Hanno, arrived on the island and marched toward Akragas as well. It would have been expected to see a combined attack on the Roman army; however, the Carthaginians remained inert. It was only in early 261, when famine began to plague Akragas, that the Punes tried to relieve the city. It was, incidentally, the first battle in which the sources mention the Carthaginians using war elephants. Those proved to be quite ineffective in combat since the combined Punic armies were unable to defeat the Roman legions. Hannibal and most of his troops managed to escape during the night, leaving Akragas to be sacked and a majority of its population to be enslaved. The failure of the Carthaginians could be blamed on their unwillingness to fight as if they hoped Rome would once again ask for peace. It is also unclear why the Carthaginian fleet didn't try to stop the Romans from transporting fresh troops to the island.

This lackluster leadership caused more disaster to the Carthaginians than just military defeats. Due to their victories, the

Romans finally decided their ultimate goal was to push out the Carthaginians from Sicily. Thus, they continued the war with more resolve than before. However, they were unable to materialize it on the battlefield. The war entered a stalemate on the land, while the Carthaginians began raiding the Italian coast from Sardinia. The raids achieved little, as plunder and prisoners were not bountiful, and they didn't hurt the Roman Republic much. Despite the raids, the Punes still didn't try to stop the Roman legions on their way to Sicily, allowing their enemy to continue putting its pressure on the land. Nonetheless, these raids finally prompted the Romans to build their own fleet. They likely realized that without it, they would never be able to fully dislodge the Carthaginians from the island. Roman historians tell us that they based their design on a Carthaginian quinquereme ship captured at Messana in 264. Those were large ships powered by five rows of oars, which had been used by the Greeks and the Carthaginians since the early 4th century. To staff them, they recruited people from their coastal allies. However, neither of their allies had much history of using a navy. It was clear to the Romans that their fleet would be inadequately matched against the savvy Carthaginian seaman.

To even the odds, the Romans invented a new device named the *corvus* (raven). It was essentially a bridge operated by swings and pullies with spikes on its end. The idea was to pull up next to the enemy vessel and drop the bridge onto its deck, with the spikes securing the connection. That would allow the superior Roman soldiers to board the Carthaginian ships and essentially defeat them in a "land" combat on the sea. It should be noted that many modern historians tend to dismiss the use of such a tool as fiction imagined by the Roman writers. In their opinion, the *corvus* was too complicated, as well as too big, compromising the ship's stability. Yet they do think the Romans most likely used some other simpler device, like grappling hooks, that would allow the legionnaires to board the enemy ships. Whatever the actual design of the *corvus* was, it proved to be extremely effective. In 260 BCE, two fleets, both numbering roughly

120 to 130 ships, met at the Battle of Mylae, located on the northeastern coast of Sicily. The Carthaginians were taken by surprise with the new Roman tactic, suffering a humiliating defeat. According to the sources, the Punes lost more than forty vessels, most of which were captured.

Interestingly, the Romans failed to capitalize on such a decisive victory, though Punic raids in Italy did stop. Instead, the Romans were satisfied with merely raiding the Carthaginian territories in Sardinia and Corsica. This prompted the Punic fleet to once again enter a naval duel with the Latins. They clashed in 258 near Sulci, a city in southwestern Sardinia, but the Carthaginians were once again defeated. The remainder of the fleet returned to Africa, where the leading admiral was crucified for his losses. Despite the naval victories, the Romans failed to conquer the Carthaginian colonies on those two islands. However, the Punes were unable to use them as a base for further raids on Italy. In contrast to the naval affairs, the Carthaginians had more success on land. After a slow advance of the Romans in 260, capturing some cities in central and western Sicily, the Carthaginians succeeded in achieving several victories. Led by a general named Hamilcar, who was not related to previous Hamilcars or the one yet to come, managed to defeat the Romans near Thermae Himeraeae in 259. Then he proceeded to capture the cities of Enna in central Sicily and Camarina, just west of Syracuse. However, that success was short-lived. By the next year, the Carthaginians were pushed back to their territories.

A 19ᵗʰ-century illustration of the Roman navy using the corvus.
Source: https://commons.wikimedia.org

Afterward, the war stalled. The Roman advance in Sicily was slowed down by long sieges, while the Carthaginians were unable to mount a new counterattack. Even worse for the Romans was their realization that the toughest Carthaginian strongholds, like Panormus (Palermo), Drepana (Trapani), and Lilybaeum, were beyond their ability to capture. Instead, they opted to follow the example set by Agathocles, to strike the Carthaginian heartland in Africa. The front remained mostly quiet, though the Romans won another naval battle in 257. By the next year, both sides amassed their navies, as it seems the Carthaginians caught wind of the Latin plans. The Roman fleet sailed to Sicily to gather the legions and sail to Africa. However, the Punes tried to stop them in a massive naval battle near Cape Ecnomus, on the southern coast of Sicily. The Roman sources most likely exaggerate the size of the forces, citing about 330 ships and 140,000 men on each side. Yet it is clear that it was a major confrontation, more massive than previous ones. The Carthaginians, led by Hamilcar, tried to employ a new tactic to counter the *corvus*, but it failed. Once again, they suffered a crushing defeat, prompting the question of why didn't the savvy Carthaginian seamen devise a counter to the *corvus*. Whatever the reason, the Punes paid the price for their military conservativism.

The Roman army soon arrived on Cape Bon, conquering the small city of Clupea to protect their landing area. The Carthaginians were unprepared for a land campaign in Africa. Thus, the Latins met little resistance at first. However, in a rather strange and unexplained turn of events, after an initial victory, the Roman Senate recalled half of the army back, leaving one consul, Marcus Atilius Regulus, with only about 15,000 men, behind to continue the African offensive. At this point, Hamilcar was recalled back to his homeland, where he met up with two more generals to stop the Roman advance. However, even with Hamilcar's five thousand men, the Punes were outnumbered. Furthermore, due to their split leadership, their army proved to be ineffective, leading to another crushing defeat. The Carthaginian hinterland was plundered, while the Berbers began rebelling once again. Facing such a crisis, the Carthaginians asked Regulus for terms of peace. Probably overconfident and thirsty for personal glory, the consul asked for the impossible. Besides the usual indemnity and release of prisoners, he demanded that Carthage leave both Sicily and Sardinia. He possibly even added terms that banned the Punes from having a military fleet while also stipulating that they couldn't make war or peace without Rome's permission. However, most modern historians tend to see those demands as yet another exaggeration by later Roman historians. Of course, the Carthaginians refused.

Despite Carthage being in a crisis and overrun by refugees, the city elders managed to gather a new army, equal in size to the Romans. More importantly, they gave the leadership over it to a Spartan mercenary named Xanthippus. With his expertise, in the spring of 255, they defeated the Romans in a battle near Tunes. It was a crushing defeat, as only two thousand legionnaires managed to get away, retreating to Clupea, where the fleet returned them home. Regulus paid the price of his hubris, as he was one of the several hundred captured Latins. His arrogance and unwillingness to connect and ally with the Berber rebels brought disaster to the African expedition. However, even worse for the Romans, the fleet returning from Clupea was caught in a storm that sunk the majority of the ships. The sources mention that about 90,000 men drowned, though that is likely another exaggeration. Nonetheless, the Carthaginians were still losing the war. While their armies were focused on subduing the Berber uprising, the Romans managed to conquer several cities in Sicily, including Panormus. The only Carthaginian victory that was achieved was the recapture of Akragas, but the Punes realized they could not keep it. Thus, they razed the city and left. By 253 BCE, Carthaginian possessions in Sicily were pretty much reduced to the well-fortified and besieged cities of Drepana and Lilybaeum, with a small stretch of land between them.

In the meantime, the Romans renewed their fleet and began raiding the African coast. However, it was a short-lived venture, as it was once again heavily damaged by a storm. After 253, there is no mention of the *corvus* anymore, prompting historians to conclude that it was no longer used due to its weight disturbing the balance of ships in bad weather. Yet the Carthaginians were unable to use this to their advantage. Their attempt to retake Panormus failed, though they did manage to subdue the rebels. By 250, the war entered a standstill. The only pieces of Carthaginian land left were the two fortified cities, which the Romans were unable to conquer. Even when the Carthaginian fleet managed to destroy almost the entire Roman navy in two battles near Drepana in 249, the situation remained the same. The Carthaginians simply exhausted their resources to field a substantial army needed to challenge the Latin legions. By 247, the only thing Carthage could afford was a small army, which was led by a new general named Hamilcar, and it went to the area around Panormus. Using guerilla-style warfare, Hamilcar tried to distract the Romans from their sieges, disrupting their supply lines with minor and fast raids. For this, Hamilcar earned the nickname Baraq, in Latin transcription Barca, meaning in Punic either "lightning" or "blessed." Yet not even his actions managed to change the course of the war.

A Carthaginian coin of the god Melqart, with the facial features of Hamilcar Barca; on the reverse is a man riding an elephant. Source: https://commons.wikimedia.org

By then, the war became a painful stalemate. The Romans were just replacing their armies, unable to conquer the two Carthaginian cities in Sicily, and instead of rebuilding their fleet, they decided to focus on reinforcing their coast. On the other hand, the Punes were mostly passive. They defended their cities, while Hamilcar's raids never grew to anything more substantial than a nuisance for the Romans. The Carthaginian fleet avoided any larger operations, content with its occasional raids on the Italian coast. The only considerable changes in those years were the Carthaginian conquests in Africa. After the rebellions were subdued, a general named Hanno, later to become known as Hanno the Great, managed to expand the Punic hinterland deeper into the continent. He conquered areas around Sicca, modern-day El Kef in northwestern Tunisia, and Theveste, today known as Tébessa in northeastern Algeria. These were fertile lands and, more importantly, new sources of tax income needed by Carthage, not only to continue its war efforts but also to compensate for the losses in Sicily. Yet even with those new sources of revenue, Carthage was both unable and unwilling to commit to any grander action in an attempt to change its footing in the war.

The standstill remained until 242 BCE, which was when Rome built a new fleet through a citizen's loan. It was once again modeled on the most advanced captured Punic vessel and manned by highly trained seamen, although it did not have a *corvus*. The fleet sailed to

Sicily, finally managing to enforce a blockade on both Drepana and Lilybaeum. It wasn't long before the defenders started to feel the effects. The Carthaginians realized something had to be done; thus, they scrambled what was left of their fleet and sailed to Sicily. In contrast to the Romans, the Punic fleet was ill-equipped. Most of their ships were old and poorly maintained, and the crews were inexperienced, as it seems the experienced seamen were unwilling to fight anymore. Further burdened by the lack of supplies, they were no match for the Latins. In 241, the Carthaginian fleet was once again destroyed in a battle near the Aegates Islands, just west of Drepana. The Romans became the unchallenged masters of both the sea and the land, while Carthage lacked the resources to try and rebuild its force. The only way out was for them to ask for peace, which they did through Hamilcar in Sicily.

The Roman terms were, of course, harsh. Carthage lost Sicily and the smaller surrounding islands, and the Carthaginians had to pay 1,000 talents upfront and another 2,200 talents over the course of 10 years. It was a hefty sum, roughly 96 metric tons of silver. No doubt that was done to prolong the recovery of the African republic. Prisoners were exchanged, and the two republics agreed not to attack each other or their respective allies. This was mostly concerning Syracuse, which remained a semi-independent ally of Rome. Finally, the treaty stated that neither side could recruit soldiers for other's land, which was more important for Rome. It wanted to preserve Italian manpower from being drained by Carthage's mercenary recruitment. However, the Latins didn't attempt to dictate what Carthage could or couldn't do elsewhere, nor did it try to ban Carthaginians from trading in Sicily or Italy. It is evident that the Romans were still eager to keep the business between them alive. Nonetheless, the war cost Carthage too much. Its treasuries were empty, her fleet destroyed, alongside its naval reputation. Carthage also lost high-income territories, and her sense of security was shattered.

After 23 years of war, the Romans managed what the Greeks couldn't for almost two centuries. They pushed the Carthaginians from their most prized possessions. This was achieved in a war that neither side particularly wanted but in which Rome showed more determination and guts. Yet, despite the losses, Carthage was still seen as a respectable power. However, her glory days were gone, and from this point onward, she began spiraling downward.

Chapter 5 – Revitalization and Demise

The First Punic War was, in every sense of the word, a disaster for Carthage. Her losses were enormous, while the gains in African expansion were rather minimal. By 241 BCE, the leading Carthaginians likely thought it couldn't get much worse, yet they were gravely mistaken.

The troubles began immediately after the war ended. About 20,000 mercenaries and Berber conscripts from Sicily returned to Africa, wanting to get paid. The Carthaginian leaders feared keeping such an unreliable foreign force near its capital, so they sent them to Sicca, along with their families. Once there, Hanno the Great tried to negotiate lowering their fees, to which the soldiers objected. Furious by such treatment and the fact that their Sicilian commander Hamilcar Barca wasn't the one dealing with them, they marched to Tunes and captured it. There, they managed to negotiate an increase in pay and secure payment for the Libyan soldiers, who weren't supposed to earn anything. However, in late 241, a coup among the mercenaries brought new leaders who were eager to wage war. They saw a defenseless enemy with bountiful plunder. The Berbers joined in, as they most likely feared retribution for siding with the mercenaries in the first place. Thus, the so-called Mercenary War began. The mercenary army quickly rose to action, while the local Libyans promptly joined in, causing widespread rebellions across

Africa. It wasn't long before they put Carthage under a blockade. Faced with such a crisis, the Carthaginian leadership reactivated Hamilcar, who had been dismissed after the First Punic War ended.

Hamilcar Barca gathered what little troops he could, broke through the mercenaries' lines, and entered the Carthaginian hinterland to reinstate control over the rebels. Using daring tactics with limited resources, Hamilcar managed to better the situation. He even persuaded the Numidian cavalry to switch sides and join him, further strengthening his army. Yet, with his focus on the Berber heartland, the rebels besieged Utica and Hippacra (modern-day Bizerte). Hanno was unable to contain them, though his presence most likely stopped them from spreading farther. Yet, by 239, both cities decided to switch sides, while the war became increasingly violent. Both sides began killing their prisoners and showed little mercy. Adding to the Carthaginian misfortune, mercenaries on Sardinia rebelled as well, managing to take over the entire island with little opposition. At that point, Hamilcar realized that the only way to defeat the mercenaries was to unite his and Hanno's army. However, by that point, Hanno and Hamilcar had become political enemies, prompting the former to refuse such an action. Hanno's reputation was already hurt by his failure, while Hamilcar once again proved to be the superior tactician and commander. As they were faced with possible insubordination, the Carthaginian authorities allowed the soldiers themselves to choose their general. They chose Hamilcar, while a more compliant commander replaced Hanno.

While the Carthaginians were preparing their counterattack, the Libyan rebels attempted to emphasize their independence by minting their own coins. These were at first used to trade with the Greeks and the Romans. The Punes attempted to stop and intercept these traders, but after the Romans protested, they stopped interfering. It proved to be an invaluable diplomatic success for Carthage, as the Latins soon banned all trade with the rebels. Also, to aid them further, they released thousands of captives from the war for free, giving a much-needed manpower boost to the Carthaginians. Hiero also sent some aid, as he realized that Syracuse needed Carthage as a counterbalance to Rome. Thus, in its dark time, two former enemies helped Carthage to survive the uprising. However, that came with a price. After the war, Rome took control of both Sardinia and Corsica. Carthage could only look on. Even though the rebellion was quelled, it wasn't in a position to do anything about it. Nonetheless, the received help signaled Carthage's reversal in the war. Hamilcar soon pressured the mercenary army enough for it to abandon its siege of Carthage, prompting it to retreat to Tunes. Despite that, he realized his army wasn't strong enough to tackle the rebels in a fortified position.

Thus, in 238 BCE, the Carthaginian army returned inland to continue its task of reasserting control over its revolting regions. A sizable rebel army foolishly followed Hamilcar on his mission. For a while, this resulted in nothing more than a series of smaller skirmishes and maneuvers, in which Hamilcar once again exhibited his ability to wage war against a numerically superior enemy. He even managed to attract some of the mercenaries back to his side. Eventually, he ambushed his pursuers, forcing them to panickily retreat into a canyon or a mountain ridge. Due to the canyon's shape, the sources name it the Saw, but historians are unsure of its exact position. Once the mercenaries retreated into it, Hamilcar shut off the exits and began starving the army. The rebels resorted to cannibalism before the Carthaginians rushed in and killed what was left of them. After annihilating a considerable chunk of the rebel forces, Hamilcar turned back to Tunes. Circumstances dictated that he and Hanno had to temporarily reconcile and work together to deal the final blow to the uprising. Working together, they managed to force the mercenaries from the city, finally crushing them all in a battle near the eastern coast of modern-day Tunisia. Most of the mercenaries died, while their leaders were gruesomely tortured before being publicly executed.

In contrast to the usual Carthaginian behavior and their treatment of the mercenaries, Carthage acted rather leniently toward the rebels. By 237 BCE, all the cities and territories were back under

Carthaginian rule, with minimal if any penalization for their uprising. It seems that this new policy toward its African subordinates included a fairer rule in the ensuing years, as those cities exhibited stubborn loyalty in later conflicts with Rome. Another significant result of the Mercenary War was that Hamilcar Barca and his party became the leading force in Carthage, ousting Hanno the Great and his followers. Immediately after the war ended, Hamilcar began planning how to restore Carthage. His first step, rather logically, was to reinstate control over Sardinia, as it still wasn't annexed by Rome. However, his attempt was halted by the Latins. They claimed the actual target of the Carthaginian fleet was Italy and declared a formal war. Carthage was in no position to challenge Rome and agreed to pay 1,200 talents for peace. It was only after this crisis that the Romans officially took control over Sardinia and Corsica. These Roman actions were clearly aimed at slowing down the economic revitalization of Carthage. The annexation of Sardinia and the declaration of formal war was seen as unjust even by the ancient writers.

Despite that loss, Hamilcar wasn't thrown off balance. He switched his focus to the Iberian Peninsula and old Phoenician colonies. Some historians have argued that Carthage had control over some Phoenician cities in Iberia even before this Spanish expedition, but there is no clear evidence for that. They may have been friendly or even allies, but it is doubtful they were under direct Carthaginian rule. However, by 237 BCE, Carthage did start to expand its influence in Spain. The sources are vague about the details, but it seems Hamilcar exploited various tactics to enlarge the Punic dominion. Some cities became allies, while others were simply conquered. Though he appears to have used brutal methods to deal with stubborn resistance in some instances, in most cases, Hamilcar acted leniently toward newly acquired lands. On his expedition, he also brought his son-in-law, Hasdrubal, who acted as his second-in-command. Hamilcar's son, the famed Hannibal, also went with them. Hannibal allegedly had to swear to his father that he would never be friendly toward the Romans to be allowed to come. Together, they extended the

Carthaginian rule over most of southern Spain, centered around the lower and middle valley of the River Baetis (modern Guadalquivir).

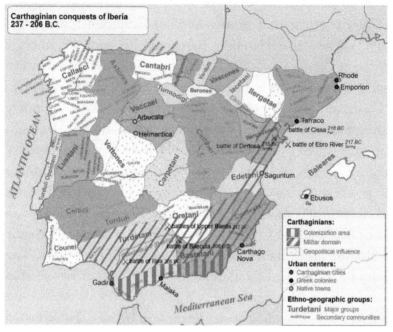

Map of Carthaginian expansion in the Iberian Peninsula.
Source: https://commons.wikimedia.org

The expansion wasn't stopped even after Hamilcar's death in a battle against an unnamed tribe in 229. He died saving Hannibal and Hasdrubal, with the latter being chosen afterward as his successor, both by the troops and the Carthaginian citizens. Hasdrubal, an acclaimed general like his father-in-law, pushed the borders of the Carthaginian dominion to the Tagus River, covering almost half of the Iberian Peninsula. The exact form of governorship across these newly acquired territories is, just like the precise details of the conquest, veiled by inconclusive sources. It is likely that local Iberian and Celtic tribes that chose to ally with the Punes had to supply them with soldiers, while those that were conquered had to pay taxes as well. The old Phoenician colonies, like Gades or Malaca (present-day Malaga), were probably only required to provide ships and crews, both for war and for transport. Of course, new Carthaginian colonies were also formed. Hamilcar founded Akra Leuke, meaning "White Cape" or "White Fort." It is unclear where it exactly stood, but modern researchers suggest it could be modern Alicante, as it would have offered an excellent link to Carthaginian Africa. More notably, Hasdrubal founded a city he named Qart-hadasht, meaning "New City." This city, today called Cartagena, was sandwiched between a safe harbor on its south and a saltwater lagoon on the north, as well as having hills behind it. It became the capital of the Carthaginian Iberian territories.

Even some of Hasdrubal's contemporaries saw it as declaring independence, especially as he began acting more like a sovereign. He also forged tighter connections with local leaders through a political marriage. He also encouraged Hannibal to take an Iberian wife. This culminated when the Spanish chiefs declared him their supreme general, *strategos autokrator*, as the Greek historians tell us. However, the evidence tells a different story. Hasdrubal, like Hamilcar before him, sent plenty of slaves, most likely captives from the conquests, as well as horses and immense wealth back to Carthage. This revitalized the Carthaginian economy and rebuilt the African provinces destroyed by the wars. It is also worth noting that the name *Qart-hadasht* was rather common for Carthaginian cities, like ones in Sardinia or eastern Tunisia. It is similar to the Greek *Neapolis*. In reality, the founding of New Carthage, as the Romans called it, proclaimed the rejuvenation of the Punic state to the Spanish people, whose loyalty Hasdrubal was working on, as well as to the Mediterranean in general. This Carthaginian renaissance was fueled not only by new tribute and taxes but also by the fact that Spain was rich with silver. Most, if not all, of the mines were owned by the state and were only leased to private contractors—a common practice across the Mediterranean and one that allowed for considerable wealth to flow into the Punic treasury.

Besides the economic advantages, Spain proved to be an important pool of manpower, a resource needed to wage a prolonged war. By the mid-220s BCE, Carthage became more of a land power, with a standing army in Iberia numbering about 60,000 infantry and 8,000 cavalrymen. In comparison, the navy had only about 130 warships, a number nearly three times smaller than at its height. The revival of Carthaginian power naturally caught the Roman eye. In around 225, an informal agreement was struck between Hasdrubal and the Latins. The Punic general promised not to advance beyond the River Iber (Ebro) in northeastern Spain. Hasdrubal only accepted the agreement because, through it, the Romans gave him tacit freedom to operate in southern Iberia as he pleased. On the other hand, it gave the Romans time to focus on their expansion into northern Italy and the Adriatic. However, circumstances began to change in 221 with Hasdrubal's assassination. His brother-in-law, who by that time had honed his military skills, became the new general and leader of Carthage. Trained from a very young age, Hannibal was a prodigious and pugnacious commander. He defeated a regional Iberian army near Toltetum, modern-day Toledo, and campaigned across central and northwestern Spain as far as the River Durius (Duero). Some of the towns and tribes he conquered himself. Others simply offered submission in awe.

*Roman statue supposedly depicting Hannibal (left) and Carthaginian coin
possibly depicting young Hannibal with symbols of the god Melqart.
Source: https://commons.wikimedia.org*

Within twelve months, Hannibal managed to almost double the
Carthaginian possessions in Spain, ruling nearly all of the Iberian
lands south of the Iber. The only exception was the city of Saguntum,
north of modern-day Valencia. By 220, the Romans noticed both
Hannibal's prowess and Carthaginian expansion. They feared that
Carthage may become too strong and that they might possibly even
expand from Spain to southern Gaul, modern-day France. That
region was not only home to Greek colonies that were friendly toward
the Roman Republic, but it was also a backdoor to Italy. Thus, they
sent an envoy to caution Hannibal not to cross the Iber as well as to
not "molest" Saguntum. This angered Hannibal, as Saguntum was
neither north of the Iber nor a Roman ally; it was merely a friendly
city. The goal of the Romans was obviously to stall his advance.
Additionally, Saguntum also acted as a good listening post for them to
keep a closer eye on the matters in Spain. However, Hannibal was not
about to buckle under such threats. Claiming that the Romans had no
business in interfering in this matter, he sent the envoy back. He

couldn't allow the Latins to exhibit enough power to meddle in Carthaginian affairs. Thus, by early 219, Hannibal besieged Saguntum, while Rome did nothing to help its supposed friends. During the entire seven-month-long siege, the Romans debated whether to act or not, with the final success of Hannibal's army swaying them over.

In the spring of 218 BCE, Roman emissaries traveled straight to Carthage, unlike before when they first went to Hannibal. After the Punic leaders refused to hand over their general, the Romans declared a formal war. The Second Punic War had begun. The war itself was avoidable, as both sides were keener on expanding elsewhere, and trade between them was flourishing. Yet the mutual mistrust and their ambitions proved to be enough to ignite another conflict. According to ancient historians, Hannibal expected it to happen. By early 218, he had his army ready. The sources tell us that Carthage had fielded about 122,000 soldiers, while Rome had roughly 71,000. However, the Roman fleet was about twice as large as the Punic one, with better-equipped ships, which was the exact opposite at the start of the First Punic War. This meant that a naval invasion of Italy was out of the question. Nevertheless, Hannibal wasn't about to wait for the Roman incursions in either Spain or Africa. Therefore, by early summer of 218, he began his march north, across the Iber toward southern Gaul. Despite his military genius, it took some time and losses to subdue the local Iberian tribes. Furthermore, upon crossing the Pyrenees, he had to send home a considerable chunk of his Spanish allies. His army dwindled to about 59,000 men, though it's worth noting that Hannibal had left much more behind in Africa and Spain.

The Carthaginian army traveled through southern Gaul away from the coast in order to avoid Greek cities allied to Rome. Most of the Gallic tribes were friendly toward the Punes, but when they arrived at the River Rhone, the hostile Volcae tried to block Hannibal's advance. He managed to defeat them with little losses. However, as they fought, Roman forces headed to Spain and landed in the city of

Massilia (Marseille) on the mouth of the Rhone. The armies were far enough apart to avoid combat, though their scouts did clash in a skirmish. Hannibal chose to eschew battle and headed toward the Alps. He had to hurry before the winter made crossing them much harder. The numerically weaker Romans didn't pursue; instead, their army continued toward Spain. Yet one of its commanders traveled back to Italy to take charge of its defense. Thus, the Romans weren't very surprised when Hannibal arrived in northern Italy in November of 218. What is surprising, and still debated among historians, is the number of his troops. Hannibal's army dwindled to somewhere around 26,000 soldiers without a viable explanation. Ancient writers attributed it to the perils of crossing the Alps, as well as the skirmishes with the local Gallic tribes.

However, the evidence points to something else. By the battle of Rhone, the Punic army had dropped to about 46,000 men. Before that, there were no battles or a lack of supplies. The only possible solution was that a number of troops deserted for various reasons, for which we have no written testimony. The losses at the Rhone were minimal, while the skirmishes on the Alps were only sporadic, causing probably even fewer losses. Furthermore, crossing the Alps during the autumn isn't as deadly as it was later romanticized. There was little snow, and they had enough supplies to not cause any substantial number of deaths, though the Punic army was far from perfect condition. Modern historians tend to ascribe these losses either mainly to desertion or to the fact that Hannibal actually began his expedition with fewer troops. Regardless of the numbers, the Carthaginian army was certainly exhausted from the march, and Hannibal knew he had to gather supplies to continue south. Thus, he first clashed with a local Gallic tribe that had resisted his proposals of an alliance. He sacked their town, modern-day Turin, and slaughtered the defenders. This not only brought him supplies but also forced other local tribes into submission while impressing Gallic tribes farther east.

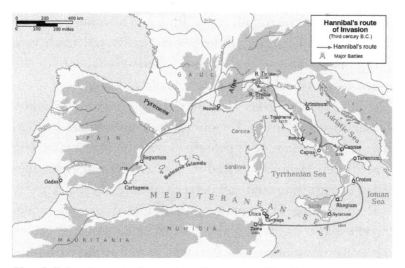

Hannibal's invasion route. Source: https://commons.wikimedia.org

By December, Hannibal began his march south, while the Romans, under the command of Publius Scipio, moved north to stop him. In a battle near the juncture of the Rivers Ticinus (Ticino) and Padus (Po), the cavalry of the two forces clashed. The Romans were beaten, and Scipio was wounded. This victory finally prompted the Gallic tribes to essentially rebel and join forces with the Carthaginians. With the Gallic reinforcements, Hannibal's army grew to about 30,000 infantry and 10,000 cavalry. Simultaneously, Scipio received reinforcements, making the Roman army similar in strength. However, the Carthaginians were superior in cavalry numbers, which Hannibal used in late December when the two armies met near the Trebia River. He used his horsemen to outflank the enemy, inflicting high casualties on the Romans. Similar to the previous battle, Hannibal released the non-Roman prisoners without a fee after the battle concluded, attempting to gather more support across Italy. He began representing himself as their liberator from Roman oppression. However, winter stopped his advance. Hannibal waited until early May, when the food was more bountiful, to continue his march south with his army, now numbering around 50,000 men, many of whom were released captives. The Romans used this time to recover from their losses, levying new legions to fight the invaders.

The Roman forces were divided into two parts, one stationed in Etruria and the other on the Adriatic coast. They wanted to block Hannibal's path with one army and possibly flank him with the other. However, Hannibal managed to slip into Etruria through the marshes of the Arno River. This took a considerable toll on his troops, while the general himself lost sight in one eye due to an infection. Once Hannibal's army arrived in Etruria, it immediately began plundering, both to gather much-needed supplies but also to force the Roman army to face them without reinforcements. At first, the Romans didn't take the bait. However, when Hannibal moved eastward toward modern-day Perugia, he forced their move. Not only did Hannibal cut off one of the armies from Rome, but he was also moving toward the second army in the east. The western portion of the Roman army immediately began the chase, while the eastern one closed in. At that moment, Hannibal exhibited his strategic genius, stopping on the shores of Lake Trasimene to set up an ambush for his pursuers. Using mist as cover, the Carthaginians descended on the unsuspecting Romans, pushing them into the water. Despite being encircled and unprepared for the battle, the legionnaires did put up a fight but were eventually crushed. About 15,000 men were killed, including the consul in charge, while another 15,000 were captured.

A renaissance depiction of the Battle of Lake Trasimene.
Source: https://commons.wikimedia.org

After the battle ended, the cavalry from the eastern portion of the Roman army arrived, as they were sent as reinforcements. Hannibal easily dealt with them, killing another 2,000 Romans and capturing about the same amount. The Romans were devastated. They expected Hannibal to besiege their capital, which was roughly four days away from Lake Trasimene. It seemed like a rather logical option, further bolstered by the fact that a new Carthaginian fleet from Africa was preparing to sail to Italy. With the combined force on the sea and land, Rome could be starved into submission. However, Hannibal chose not to do so. It was a choice for which he was criticized throughout the centuries, but his reasons were sound. He aimed to move farther south, to a more pleasant climate, to give his troops much-needed rest while cutting off the Romans from their southern allies. On top of all that, he knew that the Romans might have been defeated on land, but their navy was still operational. That made the naval blockade rather risky for the Carthaginians. For a while, the Romans were unable to do anything against the invaders, allowing them to arrive in the south uncontested. There, Hannibal tried to invoke rebellions and gain new allies but failed. However, his troops did get some much-needed respite.

This allowed the Romans time to reorganize and gather fresh soldiers. However, they changed tactics. Realizing it was unlikely to beat Hannibal in an open battle, they decided to simply tail his army and harass it. They would attack foragers, scouts, and smaller detachments. The idea was to wear out the Carthaginians without allowing them to crush the main body of the Roman army. Hannibal tried to lure them into battles, but for the most part, he failed. The only notable confrontation in almost a year was when he managed to lure one half of the Roman army into an ambush before retreating when the other half came to its assistance. Though Hannibal managed to inflict some losses, it wasn't a complete defeat of the Latin legions. Without giving Hannibal the open battle he needed, the Romans put him in a tough position. His army was getting tired, he wasn't getting reinforcements, and he couldn't achieve any notable victories to attract new allies. To worsen the Carthaginian position, the Roman army in Spain managed to achieve a significant victory over Hannibal's brother, Hasdrubal, beginning its march south of the Iber. Simultaneously, the Roman fleet raided the African coast, with the Carthaginian navy unable to stop it. By the summer of 216 BCE, the Carthaginians were in a tough position.

During that year, Roman confidence grew, while the strategy of avoiding combat with Hannibal became increasingly unpopular as a cowardly strategy both among the common population and the soldiers. This prompted the Roman Senate to authorize the consuls for that year to levy twice the usual number of legions and to finally deal with the intruder. With the allies and auxiliary troops, their combined army was about 86,000 strong, the largest Roman army up to that date. It was what Hannibal had hoped for, though, despite the discrepancy in army sizes. After some chasing around in southeastern Italy, the two armies finally met near Cannae, on the Adriatic coast of Apulia. On August 2nd, 216, the two armies clashed, allowing Hannibal to cement his legacy as a genius tactician. He knew that the Romans had more infantry, which was better equipped than most of his men, which came from the Gallic allies. However, his cavalry was better, though not noticeably numerically superior. To counter this, Hannibal arranged his infantry center in a convex line, with the additional troops on its outer end. Upon clashing with the relentless Roman legions, the Carthaginian center began to fall back in an organized manner, allowing the sides to slowly flank the advancing enemy. At the same time, his cavalry flanks managed to rout the Romans, with Hannibal's light cavalry pursuing the fleeing troops. In turn, the heavy cavalry turned back and smashed into the Roman infantry, completing the encirclement.

The Roman defeat was total. Ancient writers tell us that out of 86,000 Roman soldiers, nearly 50,000 were killed, including dozens of notable aristocrats. Another 19,000 were captured, while only 15,000 managed to escape their fates. The Roman military was crushed, totaling more than 100,000 dead since Hannibal's arrival in Italy. Once again, the Romans expected him to besiege Rome itself, yet once again, he chose not to. Modern historians often argue why he avoided attacking the heart of the Roman Republic, some claiming it was his biggest blunder and showing his lack of strategic understanding of war. Others believe that from his perspective, it made sense. Rome was too well fortified, and Hannibal lacked the equipment for a proper siege. However, it seems that Hannibal's idea of how to win a war against Rome was based on the wrong presumption that the Latins would be pressured to ask for peace at some point. Despite what later writers stated, it seems he never set out to destroy the Roman Republic, just defeat it. Hannibal sent an envoy to Rome after the Battle of Cannae to offer peace, but he was turned down. The Roman stubbornness continued afterward, despite their allies slowly defecting to the Carthaginians. Among them were not only Greek cities from southern Italy and Syracuse but also Italics, who had been granted citizenship in the Roman Republic, most notably the Samnites and Capuans.

To make matters worse for the Romans, Hannibal also formed an alliance with Philip V of Macedonia, who began attacking their territory in the Balkans. By 214 BCE, it seemed that Rome lost most, if not all, of its major allies. During all those years, Hannibal most likely expected to receive a plea for peace, yet none came. The Romans, it seems, chose to fight to the end. Even worse for Hannibal's position was the fact that the Romans returned to their previous tactics of harassment and avoidance of a head-on battle with his army, leaving him to wander across Italy seemingly without aim. As they followed him, they also began reconquering rebelled cities as well, lowering the pressure from Hannibal and replenishing their reserves. The war also expanded across the Mediterranean. Roman troops were still in Spain, where they placed pressure on Carthage, preventing Hasdrubal to reinforce his brother in Italy. Smaller detachments also fought in Sicily and Sardinia. The war expanded at sea as well, as the Carthaginians had built new fleets both in Spain and Africa. By 212, both republics had more than 100,000 active soldiers on various fronts. However, as Hannibal's sword hung above the Romans' neck, it looked like the Carthaginians still had the advantage.

Yet that soon started to change. During that year, the Romans were able to conquer Syracuse and Capua, and they threw Macedonia out of the war by allying with several Greek states. The number of Hannibal's Italian allies began to dwindle. However, in 211, his brother managed to inflict a catastrophic defeat against the Roman army in Spain, forcing them to retreat north of the Iber. Despite achieving that, Hasdrubal failed to capitalize on such a victory. Within a year, the Roman army in Spain was reinforced and placed under the command of a brilliant young general named Publius Cornelius Scipio, who was the son of the aforementioned general of the same name. He realized that the Carthaginians left New Carthage undefended, and in 209, he exploited that with a surprise attack. Conquering the center of the Carthaginian power in Spain threw Carthage off balance, and it signaled the undoing of Carthaginian control over the peninsula, with many of their allies defecting to

71

Rome. On top of that, Scipio amassed immense wealth while slaughtering the Punic population to instill fear in his enemies. Nonetheless, the Roman conquest of Spain was slow, as they faced significant resistance. Yet their advance was relentless, finally prompting Hasdrubal in 207 to lead his troops through southern Gaul and over the Alps to link up with Hannibal in Italy. It seems that they wanted to increase the pressure on Rome so its men would refocus on Italy instead of Spain.

This strategy failed miserably. Hasdrubal was defeated and killed in northern Italy before he could even hook up with Hannibal. To add insult to injury, the Romans cut off Hasdrubal's head and sent it to his brother. Hannibal was left isolated in southern Italy, and his strength was shrinking, as the last and only reinforcement he received came in 215. Over the years, Hannibal managed to win some battles, yet they were minor victories without much influence on the course of the war. As such, the main theater of the war shifted. Scipio continued his conquest of Spain, managing to inflict two major defeats on the Punic forces before finally capturing Gades in 206. By the next year, the Carthaginians lost all of their land on the Iberian Peninsula, allowing Scipio to return to Rome and plan the invasion of Africa. Mago, Hannibal's other brother, made the last attempt to prevent that from happening. He sailed from Spain with what remained of the Punic army in 205, landing in Liguria in northern Italy. However, he was too far away to join forces with Hannibal, who was attempting to secure a port in the south, to allow him to retreat. Mago managed to cause some trouble in the north before he was finally defeated in 203, succumbing to his wounds afterward.

A 19ᵗʰ-century illustration of the Battle of Zama. Source: https://commons.wikimedia.org

While the two Barcid brothers wandered in Italy, Scipio led a Roman invasion to Africa in 204, earning him the nickname "Africanus." He landed near Utica but failed to conquer it. However, he managed to defeat the Punic army and its Numidian allies twice in 203. These losses knocked the Numidians out of the war and finally forced Hannibal to return to Carthage to mount its defense. He gathered his veterans, mercenaries, and African levies to meet Scipio on the battlefield. While preparing, Hannibal attempted to negotiate peace. Still, the talks failed due to mutual mistrust, even though both Scipio and Hannibal respected each other as generals. The two of them finally clashed in 202 near Zama, almost 81 miles (130 kilometers) southwest of Tunes. It was a close battle, and at one point, it seemed that Hannibal would win. However, Scipio's cavalry managed to rout the Carthaginian cavalry and descend on the Punic rear. It was almost a reverse Battle of Cannae. Hannibal managed to get away, but by then, he realized the war was over. Upon returning to Carthage, he managed to persuade his countrymen to seek peace at any cost. In 201, the war was finally over with an overwhelming Roman victory, something that no one in 217 would have expected.

With the loss of the Second Punic War, Carthage's renaissance was over, ending as abruptly as it started. Even worse for her, the unnecessary war brought the city and its republic further down than ever before.

Chapter 6 – Succumbing to the Wounds

Losing another war against the Romans was disastrous for Carthage. After seventeen years of fighting, high expenses leaving an empty treasury, and tens of thousands lost lives, she found herself bleeding– a mere shell of a once glorious jewel of the west.

The Romans were determined not to allow the Carthaginians to rise up again. Thus, Scipio Africanus gave them terms so harsh to the point that Carthage was almost a vassal state. The Punes had to pay ten thousand talents over the next fifty years, they were banned from having a fleet of more than ten ships, and they couldn't wage war outside of Africa, while they had to seek Roman permission to do so on their own continent. In addition, the Roman Numidian allies, who had deposed of the previous ruling aristocrats who were loyal to Carthage, were given the rule over the lands of their ancestors. The issue with this clause was the fact that no clear territorial border was specified. Interestingly, Scipio didn't ask the Carthaginians to give up Hannibal, most likely since the two generals respected each other despite the vicious battles fought between them. After the terms were accepted, Scipio gathered the Carthaginian fleet in front of Carthage and ceremoniously burned it, signaling the end of Carthage's great power. Despite that, the city itself was left untouched and in control of her African territories. In fact, Scipio confirmed her existing borders before setting off back to Rome.

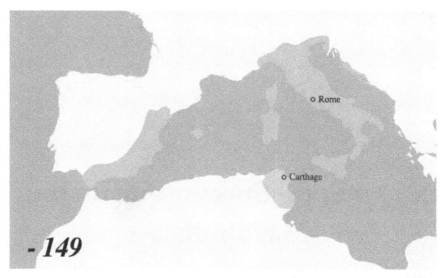

Carthaginian territory prior to the Third Punic War. Source: https://commons.wikimedia.org

Nonetheless, those African territories were in a harsh state. They were raided by Scipio and by the Roman fleet. According to later sources, Hannibal supposedly employed his soldiers to plant olive trees to help the economy recovery. Despite that, if there is any truth to the story, the Barcid party lost its grip on Carthage, and Hannibal was replaced as the leading official. However, there is no mention of Hannibal receiving any penalties for losing the war, unlike many of his predecessors in the previous centuries. Sadly, the new leading faction, most likely connected with Hanno the Great or his successors, proved to be mostly incompetent and intolerant. They wanted to impose new taxes on the citizens to help with the payment of the war indemnity. On top of that, they led Carthage in discord with Numidia, which was led by King Masinissa, a Roman ally. That was enough for Hannibal to get reelected as the leading man of Carthage around 196 BCE. Almost immediately after taking control, he showed that his talents weren't limited to the battlefield. He began an inquiry of public funds, discovering embezzlement and fraud. Hannibal managed to counter those issues by stabilizing state expenditure, even recovering some of the misappropriated funds. Furthermore, he reformed the government. The officials of the highest council in Carthage were to be chosen directly by the citizens, and they were banned from serving consecutively, though their mandates remained a year long.

Hannibal's changes made a dent in the rule of the oligarchs, but more importantly, it quickly revitalized the Carthaginian economy. The Romans immediately noticed this. Under the pretext of unresolved issues with the Numidians, in 195, they sent envoys to Carthage to supposedly settle the quarrel. Hannibal was wary of their intent, realizing the Latins likely wanted to imprison him. He knew that his position in Carthage was not as strong as before, so he simply ran. Hannibal traveled to the east, serving as a general and advisor to many kings, some of whom even fought against the Romans in later years. Hannibal died around 181 BCE without ever again playing an important role in Carthaginian history. Despite that, his reforms endured, bearing fruit to Carthage in later years. It wasn't long before the Carthaginian merchants once again started doing business across the Mediterranean. The various archeological evidence shows they traded with Italy, Spain, Greece, the Balkans, and the Azores. Their network was likely even more extensive than that. Most illustrative of their quick economic recovery was the fact that, in 191, they offered Rome to pay the remaining eight thousand talents of their indemnity at once. Despite warring in the east and needing the cash, the Romans refused, opting to leave the yearly payments as a symbolic sign of their supremacy over Carthage.

The Carthaginian offer also shows that the Punes were eager to remain on the good side of the Romans. Over the years, they acted more as trusted allies than former enemies of Rome. Only a year after their defeat, they sent a gift of 200,000 bushels of grain to Rome to aid their campaign against the Macedonians. In 191, along with the offer for the full payment of the indemnity, the Carthaginians offered a large quantity of grain, about 800,000 bushels of wheat and about 500,000 of barley, as a gift. The Romans declined the gift, opting to pay for the needed supplies. This failed donation showcases two crucial facts. One was that the agriculture of Carthage's remaining domain had recovered, while the other was that the Romans remained untrusting toward the Punes. Although many of the Latins traded and maintained connections with the Carthaginians, many still saw Carthage as a possible threat. The most famous example of this was Marcus Porcius Cato, a Roman senator, historian, and orator. He often finished his speeches with the words, "Carthage must be destroyed," even if his orations did not concern the Punes. In contrast, it seems that the Carthaginians were trying their best not to antagonize the Romans and follow the letter of their peace treaty. Most notably, they never tried to rebuild their military fleet, gather a larger army, or wage war against their aggressive Numidian neighbors.

The New City itself continued to grow, expanding to cover its once garden suburbs MEGARA, modern La Marsa. The period after the Second Punic War was also marked by public projects. Temples and palaces were being built, defenses strengthened, and most notably, its famed circular harbor known as Cothon was created. The work on the port itself may have started in the last years of the war, but it became fully functional only after the conflict ended. According to sources, it could hold 220 ships that would be protected from attacks or natural calamities. Some ancient and modern historians tried to link the construction of the harbor to an attempt to revive the Carthaginian military fleet. Yet it is more likely it was created and later expanded for commercial needs. The merchant fleet grew significantly by the mid-2nd century, following the rise in trade. The influx in trade also meant an increase in population. Modern estimates of Carthage for the first half of the 2nd century BCE usually range from 200,000 to 250,000 citizens, including the Libyan population but excluding the slaves. Without a doubt, it was still one of the largest cities of its time. The entire Punic dominion numbered around two to three million people, out of whom roughly 700,000 had citizenship rights, according to contemporary research. This meant that despite the territorial losses, Carthage still had sizable manpower potential.

Modern illustration of ancient Carthage. Source: https://commons.wikimedia.org

Despite that, the Punes, over the course of about fifty years, never tried to draw from that potential. Their chief enemy was Roman-backed Numidia, which was ruled by power-hungry Masinissa. The Roman sources are rather sketchy about details, but it seems that in the decades after the Second Punic War, on several occasions, the Numidians and the Carthaginians became involved in territorial disputes. Some were coupled with Numidian incursions, to which Carthage usually remained passive. In one instance, one of the Roman historians mentions a more significant clash between the two nations. Nonetheless, most modern historians dispute this, as the Roman reaction was too mild and tepid for it to be true. However, the Latins did usually play the role of mediators, allowing for Numidian expansion over the Carthaginian domain. Their bias was evident; around 162 BCE, they ruled that the Numidians bore more ancestral rights to the land around Leptis Magna, including the old Phoenician colony. By 151 BCE, Carthage was confined to its territories in modern northern Tunisia, as the Numidians occupied all the other African lands it once controlled. Carthage's tax income and agricultural production were halved, slowly threatening its existence. The Punes had had enough, so they gathered their troops and finally tried to oppose the Numidian attacks.

However, it was apparent that the Carthaginian army was no longer in shape to fight, as its generals lacked much-needed capabilities, and they were defeated and massacred by Masinissa's troops. It seems that the Romans brokered some kind of a truce, as the hostilities stopped. Despite that, it was reported to the Roman Senate that the Carthaginians had broken the peace treaty by waging war without its consent. Moreover, they waged it against a Roman ally. Realizing what they had done, the Punes sent their envoys to appease the Senate and avert war, but the Roman responses were vague and cryptic. While the Latins were deliberating on whether to go to war, Utica defected to the Romans, giving them an excellent base from where to begin their campaign. Since this older sister colony was ready to desert, it also signaled that the Carthaginian grip over what was left of its territory was slipping. In 149 BCE, Rome finally declared war. Their motives have been examined throughout the centuries. Some historians claimed that they wanted to exact revenge for Hannibal's destruction, others that the Romans only wanted to plunder Carthaginian wealth. Some scholars even argued that the Latins wanted to prevent the Numidians from conquering such an important city or that some of the younger generals needed a place to prove their worth. Whatever was the real incentive, the Romans sent an army of 84,000 soldiers to Africa to deal with the Carthaginians once and for all.

Realizing they had no choice, the Punes sent another embassy to Rome, offering unconditional surrender. They were ready to leave themselves at the mercy of the Latins. Unfortunately for them, the Romans had other plans. First, they asked for three hundred hostages from the leading Carthaginian families, which the Punes complied with. Then they asked for Carthaginian military supplies. The Punes surrendered no less than 200,000 sets of armor and 2,000 artillery pieces, as well as other weapons. Finally, showing their true intentions, the Roman consuls demanded that Carthage was to be abandoned and that all the Punes had to relocate ten miles (sixteen kilometers) inland. This was unacceptable to the Carthaginians, as it basically meant their destruction. At that point, the Carthaginians exploded in rage. They massacred all the Italian residents in the city, and they, too, officially declared war. The slaves were freed, while the squares and temples were turned into impromptu workshops. The entire population was involved in the war effort, illustrated by the supposed account of women cutting off their hair to make ropes for catapults. Simultaneously, the Carthaginian general Hasdrubal, who was in the countryside most likely defending it from the Numidians, was recalled to aid in the city's defense. But before he could come, the Romans marched south from Utica and besieged the city. In the meantime, the Numidians retreated to their territory, deciding not to aggravate the bloodthirsty Romans.

The war proved to be mostly one-sided, with only impregnable walls prolonging Carthage's demise. Initially, the Latin forces suffered some minor defeats and failures—most notably, their fleet was set ablaze by burning ships, which made the naval blockade of Carthage impossible for a while. The Punic army outside the city, roughly 30,000 strong, was capable only of harassing the besiegers. Nonetheless, Carthage still had some loyal cities left, most notably Hippacra, Nepheris, and Clupea-Aspis near Cape Bon. The loyalists were unable to supply their capital with troops or relieve any pressure, but they did send food and supplies. The Romans tried to capture some of these cities, mostly failing in the process. By 147 BCE, the war entered somewhat of a stalemate. The Romans continued besieging the city, but they were unable to achieve any considerable advance. More worryingly for them, their army was slowly losing its morale and discipline. On the other hand, Carthage was slowly running out of resources and was unable to inflict any noticeable damage to the invading troops. The tides of the war changed when Scipio Aemilianus, the adopted son of Scipio Africanus's son, was awarded command over the African campaign.

Upon his arrival, he tightened the siege, cutting off all land communication. Furthermore, the Romans managed to finally enact a complete naval blockade with the new fleet, along with a newly built embankment near the Carthaginian port. To make matters worse for the besieged Punes, Hasdrubal, who managed to get back to the city before Scipio arrived, became the despotic ruler of Carthage. He reportedly murdered anyone who criticized his rule, living in luxury while the citizens slowly starved. Desertions and deaths in Carthage were rising, while its defensive capabilities were lowering. During the winter, in late 147 BCE, Scipio finally managed to defeat the Punic army in the countryside, prompting all of Libya to capitulate, including the Punic loyalists such as Hippacra. The Carthaginian fate was sealed. In the spring of 146, the Romans mounted their final assault. They managed to break into the city, but they were met by fierce resistance by its citizens, who fought to defend every single house from the attackers. Here, the scenes from the fall of Motya were reenacted, with Roman and Carthaginian troops fighting on the rooftops connected by wooden planks. Eventually, the Punes retreated to the heart of Carthage, to the Byrsa citadel, to hold their final stand. On the seventh day of the battle, when the Romans began to crack down on Byrsa, what was left of the Carthaginians surrendered.

A 19ᵗʰ-century illustration of the final assault on Carthage.
Source: https://commons.wikimedia.org

By that time, only about 50,000 Carthaginians were left alive in the city, and all of them were sold into slavery. Hasdrubal, the last ruler of Carthage, surrendered as well, but his wife and children took their own lives. He was later brought back to Rome to be paraded as the defeated general. The city itself, now emptied, was razed to the ground. Everything worthy was taken, while all the buildings and walls were entirely and systematically destroyed with fire that supposedly lasted for seventeen days. While the city was burning, Scipio Aemilianus cursed anyone who might seek to once again reside in that place, finalizing the destruction of Carthage. The famous story of sowing the Carthaginian soil with salt is 19ᵗʰ-century fiction, as the sources tell us that the land on which Carthage once stood was used as public fields by local farmers. The supposed curse of the victorious

Scipio was short-lived. By the time of Caesar in the mid-1st century BCE, Carthage was rebuilt by the Romans, and it quickly rose to become one of the largest, richest, and most important cities of the Roman Empire, a center of the Roman province known as Africa Proconsularis.

Thus, the once great and powerful Carthage, the jewel of the west, ended its story in a shameful and bloody defeat. At least, that was the fate of the republic. However, the Punic culture continued to live on in the Roman state for a long time after the Carthaginians had lost their independence until it slowly disappeared from the historical stage and our collective memory.

Chapter 7 – The Carthaginian Society and Government

Usually, when talking about Carthage and the Punes, they are mentioned as a single entity, without delving deeper inside their social fabric. This is generally done for the sake of simplicity, like in the previous chapters, but also because not many surviving sources talk about this issue. Yet, to fully understand the history of Carthage, we have to take a closer look at how their state and society actually functioned.

As has been mentioned, Carthage was founded as a Phoenician colony. The creation myth of Dido, as well as the fact that Tyre and other Phoenician cities were monarchies, suggests that, in its early days, the New City was also ruled by some sort of king or monarch. However, there are no sources that tell us more about the ancient Carthaginian past. It seems that at some point, most likely during the 7th century, the Carthaginians chose to abandon the monarchical system, opting for a republic instead. Why and how this exactly happened is unknown, but by the time Greek and Roman sources write about the Punes, their state was a well-developed republic. Nonetheless, the remnants of the old monarchy can be seen through the fact that the Carthaginian state was an oligarchy, as the authority was concentrated in the hands of what we could define as an aristocracy. However, it is worth noting that the ruling elite, unlike in some other societies, was not a small and exclusive group that primarily relied on ancestry as its defining attribute. Genealogy was, of course, important to the Punes, as many took great pride in their ancestors who achieved greatness. Still, with enough talent and wealth, any Carthaginian citizen could actually become a part of the aristocracy. It is also likely that if one lacked in both, one could lose that status.

Of course, the primary condition for becoming a member of the aristocracy was to have Carthaginian citizenship. Once again, there is no clear evidence of how the Carthaginians legally or socially defined themselves. Some sources indicate that citizenship was limited to adult male indigenous Carthaginians who could theoretically link their families to the founders. This meant that women, children, and foreigners were excluded from this status. It is worth mentioning that the sources don't suggest there was a minimum wealth criterion, but it possibly existed. In addition, some scholars have argued that the Carthaginian system recognized a semi-citizenship status. Though there is no straightforward evidence for this, it has been suggested that, in some cases, it was possible to achieve a lesser citizen status, which granted some benefits of citizenship like lower taxes but possibly banned a person from rising through the governmental ranks or participating in elections. All in all, on paper, the Carthaginian citizens had the same rights and obligations. However, as throughout history and even today, inequalities stemming from birth, wealth, education, and opportunity were present. This meant that certain aristocratic families, like the Magonids and Barcids, were able to achieve longer-lasting supremacies over the state and society. Common Carthaginians could, at certain times, play essential roles in the leadership of Carthage, but it was usually under the patronage of some aristocratic family or party.

From the Greek sources, we know that the Carthaginian citizens gathered in associations or smaller groups. These were known as *mizrehims,* and their members usually bonded over communal meals, similar to the ancient Greeks. Those associations were formed based on various things. Some were focused on the following of a certain god, while others were linked to the professions of its members. There are also signs that soldiers who served in the same units also formed their own *mizrehims*. However, there is no evidence that being a member of an association was obligatory to the Carthaginian citizens, nor does there seem to be a reason for it to be compulsory. There are no explicit depictions of any other roles these gatherings had other than social bonding. The sources don't mention if they played any role in the functioning of the assembly of the citizens, yet it seems likely they played at least an unofficial role in politics. It is not unimaginable that the *mizrehims* were used by the political elites to sway the popular vote in the assembly. In some cases, that would be of the utmost importance in Punic politics, as the citizen's assembly was, in fact, the broadest form of popular rule in the Carthaginian governmental system.

Punic ruins in Carthage on Byrsa hill. Source: https://commons.wikimedia.org

The assembly was known as *ham* in the Punic language, meaning "the people." Like in the Greek cities, the *ham* gathered in the city's great marketplace, which was located southeast of Byrsa in the later centuries. How the assembly exactly functioned is unknown, as once again, surviving sources don't mention it. It has been suggested that the citizens voted in groups, maybe representing specific neighborhoods or clans, but so far, this is merely speculation. Nonetheless, it seems that through the centuries, the powers and influence of the assembly grew. The first possible mention of the *ham* is from the mid-6th century BCE when Malchus supposedly restored Carthage to its laws, treating the citizenry with reasonable respect. At the time, it seems the assembly was still more of a voice of the people than a genuine part of the governmental system. Later on, it gained the right to elect magistrates and government officials. Yet by the time of the Barcids and the Second Punic War, the assembly of the citizens had the power of ratification, at least to a certain degree, on the decisions made by the upper assemblies of the state. Aristotle also conveys that the *ham* was a place of debate, not only voting, praising the democratic nature of the Carthaginian government. Of course, it should be noted that the ancient notion of democracy is far different and less liberal than our modern ideals.

Yet, like in many modern republics, Carthage also had a small high council, usually called by its Roman name, the senate. In the Punic language, its name was *adirim*, roughly translated to "the great ones," invoking a feeling that this governmental body was superior to the *ham*. This authority most likely came from the fact that the *adirim* was the oldest governmental assembly. It seems it existed since the monarchical era, at first functioning as the king's advisory council of leading men of the city. Though there is no clear evidence for it, the historians think it is rather likely that the senate was responsible for ending the monarchy and instituting the republic, thus giving the *adirim* the theoretical supremacy in the state. Its influence was only greatened by the fact that all of its 200 to 300 members were from aristocratic families, though how they were precisely chosen is unknown. The *adirim*'s authority seems to have been rather broad. From the sources, we know that it was tasked with diplomatic decisions, matters of war and peace, treaties, etc. Its members also acted as judges, while the surviving sources hint at the fact that the *adirim* also played a role in the internal affairs of the state. However, like the *ham*, the sources don't mention how the *adirim* exactly functioned, leaving yet another aspect of the Carthaginian governmental system in the dark.

Besides the *ham* and the *adirim*, the Carthaginian state was also ruled by the *suffets*. The *suffets* were an annually elected pair of chief officials. The name we use for them is a Latinized version of the Punic *shophetim* or *shuphetim*, which is usually translated as "judge." Historians have concluded, though not with substantial evidence, that the *suffets* most likely existed in the form of actual judges in the time of the monarchy. Yet when the republic was instated, the *adirim* transformed the office into one of the high magistrates. It has been suggested that in the early days of the republic, there was only one *suffet*, but this cannot be proved. If that was the case, by later periods, two became the norm. Their authority was mainly executive, though it seems that at certain times they also proposed laws or decrees to the *adirim*. The remnants of the judicial roots of the *suffets* also remained as, in some instances, they presided in civil lawsuits. Yet, like other aspects of the Carthaginian government, much about the *suffets* remains shrouded in mystery. The exact nature of the high magistrate office has only been made more convoluted by the fact that that the Greek writers usually called them kings (*basileis*), even when Aristotle talks about them as elected officials. In turn, the Romans have used their terms, such as consuls or praetors, when talking about the *suffets*, inferring at least some similarities between them.

What seems to be certain is the fact that wealth and ancestry were a requirement for the office. However, there are no details about how much capital was required or how the distinction of birth was defined. From the sources, the scholars have deemed that in the early days of the republic, it was most likely the *adirim* who chose the *suffets*, but in later periods, at least from the 4th century BCE, this power was transferred to the *ham*. This was a sign of gradual democratization of the Carthaginian government, which was praised by the Greeks and condemned by the Romans. In fact, Aristotle, writing in the 4th century, admired the Carthaginian system as one in which the ideals of a monarchy, in the form of the *suffets*, an oligarchy, in the form of the *adirim*, and a democracy, in the form of the *ham*, intertwined, balancing each other out. However, this democratization was not intentional, nor was it fueled by some idealistic altruism or liberalism. The main power behind such developments was the fact that in the earlier republic, when the *suffets* and the *adirim* clashed, the *ham* broke the tie. Over time, the opinion of the people became more important, leading to the involvement of a broader public into political decisions. By the end of the Second Punic War, the Carthaginian government was democratized enough for the *ham* to vote in every major decision made by the other two groups. It was democratized enough for Polybius, a Roman historian and contemporary of the war, to deem that the Latins won because of their superior aristocratic political system.

Apart from these three central bodies of the Carthaginian governmental system, sources give us glimpses of other lesser offices, though they mainly remain opaque and mysterious. Aristotle mentions an institution of "pentarchies" or five-man commissions that delved into judicial and other vital matters. Beyond this, we have no other mentions of them. Still, the Carthaginian state likely had a number of commissions and bureaucrats who were appointed for a longer period, serving the state apparatus. The Punic inscriptions hint at the existence of commissions for sacred places and for supervising taxes, though none numbered exactly five members. Those inscriptions also attest to the existence of treasurers or accountants, *mehashbim* in Punic, who dealt with the enforcement of tax payments. Above them stood a head treasurer, the *rab*, meaning "chief" or "head," who was in charge of the state finances. It seems likely that the *mehashbim* were his subordinates, but unlike them, the *rab* was a position with a time limit, most likely constrained to a year. Of course, the mentioned commissions and offices were probably only a part of the Carthaginian apparatus, but so far, there has been no evidence to shed more light on its complexity. The only additional details that we have is that one person was banned from holding two offices at the same time, like simultaneously being a *suffet* and a *rab*.

As for the nature of the Carthaginian political scene, we can see from many sources that corruption and misuse of held positions were rather prevalent, at least until Hannibal reformed the state after the Second Punic War. Besides that, we know that the Carthaginians were often divided into two or more political factions, usually centered around one leader, but they weren't officialized as parties like in modern republics. They were more fluid and everchanging. The struggle between factions was sometimes so high that they put the survival of Carthage at stake, though in some cases, all differences would be set aside to assure the New City wouldn't fall. The contested political landscape was only further complicated with military offices. Martial functions in the Carthaginian republic were separated from the civil offices, unlike the Roman state. The highest of them was *rab mahanet*, translated simply as general. However, despite the official segregation, it was possible to hold military and governmental positions at the same time. It wasn't unheard of that the *suffets* were also awarded military commands. Along with the disjunctions of offices came a military tribunal, known as the Court of One Hundred and Four. Additional details about the military branch of the Carthaginian republic will be given in the subsequent chapter about the Punic army.

A 19th-century painting of Carthage. Source: https://commons.wikimedia.org

One thing is somewhat noticeable when looking at the entire Carthaginian government and politics. It does revolve quite openly around wealth. Whether it was about having enough of it to apply for the top state offices, being rich enough to be counted as part of the ruling aristocracy, or using it for simple bribery and corruption, the Carthaginians seemed to have been quite fond of money, orientating their entire state toward earning it. This goes rather well with the notion of the Carthaginians being primarily merchants interested only in profit and nothing else. However, these are mostly modern exaggerations, as the ancient sources rarely dwelled on such topics, focusing more on warfare and politics. Despite that, the Greek and Roman sources do praise the mercantile capabilities of the Carthaginians, giving an honorary title of the wealthiest city in the world to Carthage in several texts. Thus, despite supposedly having a merchant-run oligarchical republic where trade was everything, no surviving sources touch on the topic of the Carthaginian traders except a single Roman comedy. In *Poenulus* (*The Little Carthaginian*), a Punic merchant named Hanno is traversing the Mediterranean in search of his long-lost daughters. The plot itself is less important, but in the play, Hanno is shown trying to sell various cheap items like pipes, ladles, lard, spades, nuts, and even "African mice." Through this comic representation, we are shown that the Carthaginians would trade in anything as long as it would turn a profit.

Though an exaggeration, this description in recent years has become increasingly accepted as plausible. The archeological evidence shows that the Carthaginians traded a wide variety of goods, from raw materials to finished products. In their wares, one could find various precious metals, like silver and gold, but also tin, copper, iron, animal skins, ivory, wool, amber, and incense. They also traded in foodstuffs like olives, olive oil, wine, cereals, salted fish, spices, herbs, and garlic. The crafted goods were also as variable as the raw products, including, among others, embroidered textiles, purple-dyed cloth, food utensils, various tools, furniture, jewelry, ceramics, eating utensils, glassware, and even weapons. This made the Carthaginians among the most versatile traders of their time, especially when we take into account the fact that they sold not only high-grade products but also cheaper low-grade items. They used them to trade with less-developed tribes in Iberia and Africa or anyone else willing to buy them. With that in mind, Hanno's fictional stock is more realistic than it would seem initially. Combining the archeological and written sources, it becomes clear that the Carthaginians were indeed avid traders, making it quite intriguing that they began minting coins only in the late 5th and early 4th centuries BCE.

Considering the coinage spread throughout the Mediterranean from the 6th century, this was a relatively late development for an advanced state like Carthage. However, this can be explained by the fact that most of their dealings were done with less-developed societies in the western Mediterranean, thus leaving them to use barter and weighed pieces of precious and semi-precious metals in trade. Herodotus claims they only accepted gold, but this seems like yet another exaggeration. The fact that the first coins were minted to be used as payments for the mercenaries proves that the barter economy was still functional for the Carthaginians even in the early 4th century. It also goes to show that the Carthaginian state was not run as a trading company by merchants merely trying to achieve a profit. However, the state did try to protect its own traders, both from the pirates and foreign competition. Carthage protected the former with its military fleet, while the latter it tried to achieve with trade agreements like it had with Rome in 509. It is also worth noting that there were state-run business ventures, but it is hard to distinguish between them and private endeavors, as many of the wealthy merchants were a part of the government.

Nonetheless, not all the aristocrats were merchants, or at least not entirely. From the early 5th century BCE, when Carthage began its expansion in the African hinterlands, the class of landowners also emerged. It is important to mention that there was a clear distinction between Carthage's city-territory that consisted of its immediate hinterlands, including Tunes and the Cape Bon Peninsula, subjected Libyan lands, and the territory of its African allies. Despite that, nothing barred the Carthaginians from owning property in all three areas. By the late 3rd century, the sources mention that the city-territory was developed enough to provide the Carthaginians with their needs, while the taxes from Libya covered the expenses of the state. That meant that the immediate hinterland of the city was capable of feeding its entire population, which numbered about 650,000 at the time. This coincides with the fact that Aristotle, as well as other ancient writers, praised the Carthaginians for their agricultural expertise, depicting their bountiful fields and filled granaries. This reached a point where a manual on estate management, in effect, a complete encyclopedia of farming, which was written by a retired Carthaginian general in the 4th century, was so acclaimed that the Romans saved it for themselves after the destruction of Carthage. Unfortunately, its text survives only as excerpts in the works of later Roman authors.

In those passages, the workers are mentioned, who, in fact, constituted a significant part of the Punic society. Among them were, of course, non-citizens, foreigners, and slaves but also common

Carthaginians. Many of them were unskilled laborers like dockworkers, porters, or other physical workers. However, the exact relations between employers and workers, and their wages, are still much of a mystery for modern scholars. Above them were skilled artisans, producing various goods from tools and pottery to finer jewelry and glasswork. The expert craftsmen were so sought after in Carthaginian society that it has been suggested that foreign workers were possibly given the aforementioned semi-citizenship. This also refutes the usual depictions of Punes as mere middlemen in trade. Many of the goods they sold were made by their artisans and were, in fact, much sought-after in the Mediterranean world. Apart from the craftsmen, other skilled professions existed as well, like scribes, teachers, architects, and doctors, which were all needed to keep a bustling city like Carthage working. It was common for workers of the same trade to live in a specific area in the town, forming guilds to protect and improve their business. Of course, like the landowners, not all of them were rich and respected or owned a large workshop. Most of them lived thriftily in tightly packed neighborhoods in simple homes, some even living in multi-storied buildings, which would have housed several families.

On the margins of the Carthaginian society were two noticeable groups. One such group was the foreigners, who were always present in a cosmopolitan city like Carthage. They came from all over the Mediterranean, looking for their fortune in various ways. Like in many ancient societies, they were always clearly separated from the local population. However, the citizens of Carthage's allies were possibly treated somewhat better, at least having the same legal rights and once again conceivably falling in the semi-citizen category. The other marginalized group was women. Not much is known about their position in society, as sources remain almost dead silent about them. As mentioned, they were banned from having citizenship, which is in line with other ancient republics like Rome and Athens. This suggests that they lacked the legal rights of male Carthaginians, not to mention that they were surely not allowed to delve into the world of politics.

Some women are mentioned in the temple dedications but never alone. They were always mentioned with their fathers, husbands, or brothers. Also, there are no records of women owning any businesses or properties. All that combined indicates, though not proves, that the majority of, if not all, women were unable to own anything. It seems that despite having a princess, Dido, as their founding figure, the Carthaginians, like most ancient societies, treated women as second- or even third-class members of their community.

A 19th-century illustration of Carthaginian women. Source: https://commons.wikimedia.org

The only group that had it worse than women were, of course, the slaves. Like in other ancient societies, the Carthaginians deemed slaves as a regular part of everyday life. A number of them were prisoners of war, but one could be enslaved for an unpaid debt or traded in the markets as a commodity. If a child was born to slave parents, it would also become a slave. The life of the slaves was no doubt harsh, but there are some indications that the Carthaginians treated some of them with a bit more leniency than was usual in the ancient world. The already mentioned manual on farm management suggests that one should not be too harsh on slaves in order to inspire loyalty and better productivity as a result. In other sources, we hear of slaves actually running businesses for their masters, amassing enough wealth for temple dedications or even gaining their own freedom. Though, it should be noted that even when freed, slaves were never fully integrated into society. In turn, except for the previously mentioned two major revolts, the Carthaginian slaves proved to be quite loyal, even fighting until the end alongside their masters in 146. That being said, it shouldn't be imagined that the life of the Carthaginian slaves was much better than in other societies of that time. Not everyone followed the instructions of the farm manual, and the slaves, regardless of that, lacked basic human rights, not to mention other aspects that make life worth living.

With all that has been said in this chapter, it is clear that the Carthaginian society had some unique traits, while others fit perfectly into the mold set by other better-known ancient civilizations. Yet the most glaring fact is that much about the Carthaginians remains a mystery still to be uncovered from the fog of time.

Chapter 8 – Army of the Carthaginian Republic

Even though the Carthaginians were never really considered to be a militaristic or warmongering state, warfare proved to be a significant part of their history. They often fought wars to preserve their dominance and expand their sphere of influence. Because of that, their army, despite not being the most impressive one in the ancient world, deserves a short overview as well.

At the head of the Punic army stood the *rab mahanet* (general), who was elected as a governmental magistrate, separating civil and military duties in the governmental system. This office proved to be more flexible than others, as the length of service was not fixed. One would serve as a general until the war was over or until he was recalled and substituted by another commander. Also, the number of active *rab mahanets* could vary depending on the needs of Carthage. In smaller conflicts, it was usually one or at most two commanders appointed, but in the Second Punic War, up to seven men, mostly from the Barcid family, held ranks of generals. It is also worth noting that generals also commanded the navy; there was no separate admiral rank title. However, a deputy or a second-in-command existed in some cases, holding the title of the *rab sheni*, roughly translated to "second general." Usually, generals had full autonomy in deciding the course of action, both in military and diplomatic decisions, though in some instances, the *adirim* or the *ham* needed to ratify peace treaties or truces. Another issue that sometimes came up was when two equally ranked generals led armies in the same area, raising the question of who held the higher command. It is also important to note that generals were always held accountable for their actions, with harsh penalties hovering above their heads.

In the early days of the republic, it seems that a general's competence was judged by the senate or some of the lesser commissions. However, by the late 5th and early 4th centuries, a special military tribunal was formed. Known as the Court of One Hundred and Four, it was supposedly the highest authority in Carthage. The number of members was deemed odd by modern historians, with some claiming it was more likely around one hundred. However, it's more likely that it constituted the one hundred members of the *adirim* and the four principal magistrates that were active. Once again, the question on how the judges were precisely chosen remains a mystery apart from Aristotle informing us it was based on merit. At first, the Court of One Hundred and Four was given authority over only the generals, but over time, it began to widen, allowing for subordinate officials to be judged as well. By the late 3rd century, it seems that the court began to infringe on other bodies' functions, instituting a somewhat despotic rule over Carthage. This was cut short by Hannibal's reforms, reducing the membership in the court from a life term to a single year.

Regardless of those reforms, the intended role of the One Hundred and Four to keep the generals in line and in the service of the senate and the people remains questionable. Most of the generals and members of the court were also aristocrats and members of the *adirim*. Thus, an accused general would be tried by his political enemies and allies, leading to a high possibility of a politicized tribunal that had little to do with merit or competence. In addition, as the court had the right to execute the failed generals, usually in a gruesome fashion like crucifixion, it was a perfect constitutional platform to get rid of possible political rivals. Additionally, such pressure also backfired on many Carthaginian generals, prompting them to remain passive and overcautious, afraid of the repercussions of failure. In some cases, the defeated generals opted to take their own lives instead of waiting for the trial in front of the One Hundred and Four. Nonetheless, despite all its shortcomings, the Court of One Hundred and Four proved to be a long-lasting and quite important feature of Carthaginian military and political life.

Illustration of a Carthaginian hoplite and a Carthaginian horseman.
Source: https://commons.wikimedia.org

The organization and structure of the Carthaginian army also passed through several stages throughout its history. In its earliest history, it was likely shaped upon the Eastern models, most likely following the Assyrian archetype. However, by the 6th century, the Carthaginians began reshaping their army according to the Greek model, basing their military upon the heavy spearmen in phalanx formation. At the time, the majority of soldiers were citizen recruits who were conscripted by the state. However, during the 5th century, the Carthaginians slowly began turning toward mercenaries. At first, they were just additional troops, but by the 4th century, they became the primary fighting force. This was done most likely to preserve the population of Carthage, which, despite its relative size, was unable to withstand prolonged wars with higher casualties. However, it seems that in most cases, the Carthaginians tried to retain their own officers among the mercenaries to ensure their loyalty. The mercenaries were recruited from all over the Mediterranean, most commonly from their African and Iberian domains, as well as southern Gaul, Greece, and southern Italy. It seems that the Greeks were especially valued, as in some cases during the 3rd century, their captains were given commands over the entire Carthaginian army due to their expertise.

In turn, this brought another change to Carthaginian warfare. Influenced by the Greek commanders, the Carthaginians accepted the Hellenistic combined arms model, which no longer relied solely on the phalanx. The new style also utilized both light and heavy cavalry, as well as the light infantry and skirmishes. In addition, the Carthaginian army also used war chariots and elephants. This made the Punic army much more versatile and adaptable, which was more suited for the wars with Rome, as they were on a much larger scale and broader fronts than the ones with the Sicilian Greeks, which was led mostly on a single island. Honed by the long Punic Wars, by the end of the 3rd century, the Carthaginian army was no longer a mishmashed group of mercenaries gathered for a shorter altercation. It became more of a standing army with experienced commanders at its head. However, after the loss of the Second Punic War, the Carthaginian domain shrank, as well as its monetary power, leading to the downsizing of its military. There were fewer and fewer mercenaries, and once again, Carthage had to rely more on its citizens, though, in the last fifty or so years of its existence, the Carthaginians tried to avoid major conflicts. By the end of the Third Punic War, the Carthaginian military became a citizen militia, even aided by the slaves, as they tried and failed to ward off the Roman legions.

Due to its mostly mercenary basis, the Carthaginian army was quite fluid in composition, not always consisting of the same types of troops. However, throughout most of its history, an elite formation consisting of young aristocrats existed. The Greeks called it the Sacred Battalion, though no Punic name is mentioned. It consisted of about 2,500 young nobles trained in the Greek phalanx formation and equipped with the best quality armor. Prepared from a young age, they were said to be quite disciplined—the best Carthage could field. However, their track record was not that impressive. It seems that despite their drills, professional Greek soldiers were able to outmatch them in most cases. This may come from the fact that the Sacred Battalion was only fielded in times of crisis and quite rarely outside of Africa. That meant they fought mostly in tough battles against enemies who were stronger than usual. Besides the Sacred Battalion, other Carthaginian citizens usually served as heavy cavalry and officers, most of them also from wealthier classes. Their numbers were limited, serving mostly to ensure loyalty and discipline among the mercenaries and levied troops. In later periods, when citizens once again became prominent in the infantry, they used the Hellenistic phalanx as their basis. However, it's fair to assume they were not as viable as the Sacred Battalion was.

Other soldiers that served in the infantry were mercenaries from across the Mediterranean world, most of which also formed phalanx formations. Thus, they carried long spears, round shields, metal helmets, and tunics, as well as short swords and greaves. Some of the Celtic and Iberian tribes also provided skilled swordsmen, with the former preferring the long sword and the latter the short sword. Among the Libyan tribes, some preferred double-headed axes, as well as crescent-shaped shields. Interestingly, women warriors were also mentioned among those African mercenaries. How many, if any, were present remains a question, though. Archers were also deployed, like the expert Moors and Cretans, but in far lesser number than in most other armies. Among the ranged units, the Balearic slingers were especially distinguished. They were famed for the precision of their slingshots, making them perfect for initial skirmishes and harassment of enemy lines. However, for harassing enemies, the preferred type of troops among the Carthaginian generals were the light cavalry. These soldiers were also mercenaries, usually equipped with lighter armor, javelins, and short swords. They were capable of maneuvering across the battlefield easily, making them more versatile than the heavy cavalry of the Carthaginian aristocrats, which usually could only dive straight into the enemy lines. The Numidians were considered the best light cavalry, followed by the Iberians and Moors.

Some of the Carthaginian mercenaries: Balearic slinger (left), Iberian infantry (center), and Numidian cavalry (right). Source: https://commons.wikimedia.org

Other mounted units were used as well. War chariots were used up to the 3rd century before being abandoned as too impractical for any terrain apart from flat open fields. The chariots usually had two-man crews, with a driver and an archer or spear thrower. With scythes on the wheels, they were supposed to crash into the enemy lines, causing disarray and panic. However, they mostly failed in their role as mobile field artillery, leading to them being replaced by the famed war elephants of Carthage. The Carthaginians used now-extinct North African elephants (*Loxodonta africana pharaohensis*), which were smaller than its living African cousin. Reaching only about eight feet (2.5 meters), these animals were likely not large enough to carry a wooden tower as the Indian war elephants did. Still, they were capable of carrying one rider and one archer. However, this assumption has been widely debated as they were often depicted as having a tower on their backs, leaving scholars without any conclusive decision. Regardless of that, the main goal of the war elephant was the same as the chariots. They were to charge the enemy lines and create gaps for infantry and cavalry to exploit. Adding to the fact that they had long tusks, maybe even adorned with additional spears, the elephants were, if anything, a psychological weapon capable of inflicting fear into Carthage's enemies.

Despite being rather famous for the use of elephants, especially after Hannibal crossed the Alps with them, the war elephants in Carthaginian warfare proved to be rather ineffective. When they fought against well-trained enemies, like the Roman legions, the elephants were unable to instill fear, especially after the first surprise encounter. Even worse, they were known to get frightened or anxious and turn on the Carthaginians themselves. Additionally, like the chariots, the elephants had trouble fighting on non-flat battlefields. Thus, the war elephants proved to be more of a symbol than functional mobile field artillery. In contrast, the regular siege artillery of the Carthaginians was rather useful. Those were mostly used in the wars in Sicily, as most of the cities there were well-fortified. In this aspect, the Carthaginians once again learned from the Greeks, adopting their catapults and crossbows. Less sophisticated weapons were also used, like battering rams and siege towers, while tactics of mining and building mounds were employed to bypass enemy walls. Besides using the artillery for offensive purposes, the Carthaginians used them for defense as well. They at least equipped their own capital with artillery weapons to add an additional deterrent to possible invaders.

Another important part of Carthaginian warfare was the tactics they used. In the earlier days of employing the Greek hoplite formation, it is likely they used a similar straight-on tactic of the Greeks. A wall of hoplites would directly clash with the enemy, where their raw strength and endurance were the key elements. In such clashes, there was little maneuvering, and if some were capable of outflanking the enemy, it usually proved to be decisive. However, with the later development of the Hellenistic combined warfare, it was this maneuvering that became vital for victory. Despite that, the heavy phalanx infantry, which was lacking in maneuverability, remained at the center of the Carthaginian army. With its high defensive capabilities, it was there to take on the brunt of the enemy attacks. The lighter infantry was on its immediate flanks, protecting them while also trying to flank the enemy. On the outer flanks stood the cavalry. Its first task was to harass the enemy lines before either clashing with enemy horsemen or trying to outflank the enemy army. The heavy cavalry was also sometimes used to break the enemy's formation. Moreover, the cavalry was occasionally used to set up ambushes and attack from behind. Yet, with the use of Hellenistic warfare, the battles became less predictable, and the tactics varied depending on the circumstances, making this description of Carthaginian tactics less of a rule and more an oversimplified generalization.

Finally, when talking about the Carthaginian army, its fleet also needs to be mentioned. According to the ancient sources, at its height, the Punic armada numbered about 350 warships. Those were large ships, powered by both sails and oars, with two steering oars on both sides of the stern. Although some historians argue if both rudders were used simultaneously, ancient sources hint at this. It possibly explains why they considered the Carthaginian ships to be the most maneuverable on the battlefield. As for the armaments, the Carthaginians principally used bronze rams mounted on the prow, below the surface, using it to puncture enemy vessels. Unlike land warfare, in the naval battles, there were usually two simple overall tactics, one in which the ships tried to ram the enemy head-on. In the other, a flanking maneuver would be attempted. Different tactics were possible but less common. In battles, the oars were the primary source of propulsion, allowing for more reliable and consistent speeds. However, it was also important not to penetrate the enemy ships too much, as it could lead to a Carthaginian ship getting stuck. It is worth noting that these tactics were not solely used by the Carthaginians, as it was a common way of fighting among the civilizations of the ancient Mediterranean.

In addition to ramming, it was also commonplace to use javelins or other missiles against foes. However, unlike the Romans, the Punes avoided boarding enemy ships. Heavier artillery was usually avoided, as it made the vessel unstable, even in later periods when the vessels were larger. Early in Carthaginian history, the primary type of ship used was a trireme, named after having three rows of oars on each side. These were no small vessels, though. They fit 180 rowers, plus additional crew members, and the ship itself was usually about 120 feet (37 meters) long and about 16 feet (5 meters) wide. The origins of the trireme, used across the Mediterranean, are disputed. Some researchers claim the Carthaginians themselves developed it, while others ascribe it to their Phoenician brethren. However, as time went by, the idea of making larger ships that were more impervious against ramming drove the Punes to be the first one to develop the quadrireme, a larger version of a trireme with four rows of oars. Eventually, a quinquereme, a ship with five rows of oars, was developed by Dionysius of Syracuse, but it was quickly adopted by the Carthaginians, becoming their primary type of battleship. It was about 147 feet (45 meters) long, 16 feet (5 meters) wide at water level, while its deck was around 10 feet (3 meters) above the surface. It required about 420 seamen to fully man it, out of whom no less than 300 were rowers.

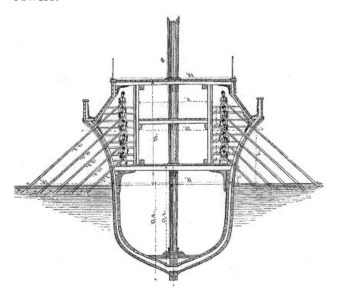

A 19ᵗʰ-century diagram of a quinquereme ship. Source: https://commons.wikimedia.org

The crews of the Carthaginian ships were, unlike the ground forces, made up almost exclusively of the Punes themselves. Though mostly from the lower classes, the Carthaginian seamen were considered among the best in ancient times due to their extensive training. This was only helped by the fact that many of the Punes were already familiar with the sea as merchants. However, it's worth noting that in the last two hundred years of Carthaginian history, their navy had lost its edge from inactivity. The majority of the crew were rowers, who, besides rowing, were expected to take arms and fight if the ships were beached or boarded by the enemy. Additionally, there were marines and archers, trained soldiers whose sole purpose was to fight. Above all of them were three officers, one of whom was the navigator. Above them stood only the chosen admiral of the entire fleet. The fleet itself had a variety of purposes. During peacetime, it safeguarded Carthaginian merchants both from pirates and from competitors that were supposedly trespassing into Carthaginian waters. In times of war, besides fighting off the enemy navy, the fleet also served for transporting armies and supplies, raiding the enemy coast, and aiding in sieges through naval blockades. Additionally, they could disrupt the enemy supply convoys and even relieve and resupply besieged Carthaginian cities or forces.

All in all, when considering all the facts, the Carthaginian army, both its ground and naval forces, proved to be one of the better ones of ancient times. If nothing else, it was one of the rare forces that were able to knock on the doors of Rome itself. Despite that, only a handful of its components originated in Carthage but were instead imported from other places, both in manpower and in technology and tactics. That was a two-sided blade. It allowed the Carthaginians to follow the best military trends. Yet, once it stopped evolving, their army and navy quickly became obsolete. In the end, that was what happened. During their clashes with the Greeks, they were willing to learn from their enemies, adopting the hoplite formation as well as the later Hellenistic type of armies. However, after clashing with the Romans, the Carthaginians were not quick enough to realize the advantages of the Roman style of warfare, leading to their ultimate demise.

Chapter 9 – The Punic Civilization

Often when talking about Carthage and the Punes, the focus is solely on their wars against Rome and the Greeks, maybe on their mercantilism and economy as well. Yet it is rare to delve on the topic of their culture and religion; it is almost as if that aspect of their society is less important or, even worse, nonexistent. However, the truth is that the Punes had quite a developed civilization that is worthy of our attention.

One of the most important aspects of Carthaginian culture was no doubt their religion, like in all other ancient societies. Like many others throughout history, the Punes believed in a multitude of gods. The basis of their pantheon was the Phoenician one, as the early settlers brought their old beliefs with them. However, not much is known about the exact mythology behind the gods. We do know which were the most respected deities, like, for example, Melqart and Baal and his many incarnations. Melqart was originally the god protector of Tyre, a role which he most likely had in Carthage as well. Later on, the Greeks saw Heracles (the Roman Hercules) in him, leading to a cult of Melqart-Heracles spreading across the Mediterranean. As a hero-god, many generals, including the Barcid family, worshiped Melqart keenly. Baal was the chief god, like Zeus or Jupiter, but he had many incarnations that may have been praised as separate deities. In Carthage, Baal Hammon was the chief god, as well as the god of weather and fertility of vegetation. Other important gods were Eshmun, the god of renewal and healing; Reshef, the god of fire; and Rasap, the god of war. Less significant Phoenician deities in the Punic religion were Semes, the sun goddess; Hudis, the god of the new moon; Kese, the god of the full moon; Hawot, the goddess of the dead; and Kusor, which had a female form of Kusarit, god/goddess of intelligence.

Yet not all deities were directly taken from the old Phoenician religion. For example, a major Carthaginian goddess, Tanit, which in later periods surpassed both Melqart and Baal in importance, was most likely not worshiped in Phoenicia. Her origins are disputed, as some researchers argue the Punes created her. In contrast, others trace her beginnings as an insignificant servant of the Phoenician goddess Astarte. Often coupled with Baal, Tanit was the goddess of fertility, life, and motherhood. She is also the only Carthaginian deity that had her own symbol, at least that is known today. It was a triangle with a horizontal line and a sphere above it, a stylized representation of a woman in a dress spreading her arms. Besides the Phoenician and original Punic deities, the Carthaginians also accepted gods of other neighboring nations. Among more prominent ones were the Greek Demeter and Persephone, whose worship began in 396 BCE after the Carthaginians burned their temple in Syracuse, which was seen as the cause for the ensuing disasters that followed. Another borrowed deity was the Egyptian Isis, which came through close trading relations among the two nations. Other gods were surely worshiped, though. Some may have been brought by the immigrants and settlers that came to Carthage during its long cosmopolitan history, yet their existence is unclear. The Greek and Roman sources tend to call all Punic deities with the names of their gods, making it hard to decipher the exact Punic pantheon.

A 4ᵗʰ-century bust of goddess Tanit (left) and symbol of Tanit on a stele (right).
Source: https://commons.wikimedia.org

Likewise, there is little information on the theology and practice of religion among the Carthaginians. They had a multitude of temples, likely resembling the old Phoenician sanctuaries with two large columns, one on either side of the entrance, leading into a three-chambered interior. Inside it would be a large bronze bowl with an eternal flame instead of a representation of a particular deity. Religious life was maintained by a number of priests, known as *kohanim*, led by a head priest with the title of *rab kohanim*. He was possibly linked with preserving the cult of Melqart and performing yearly death and rebirth rituals of this god. The higher priestly titles were reserved for the aristocratic families and were considered quite significant. The *rab kohanim* was even a member of the *adirim*. Beneath him were chief priests of particular temples, who would have been aided by lesser priests. It has been suggested that female priestess also existed, but their role and importance is unknown. However, it seems that the temples were off-limits to common women. In addition to the religious functions, the priests may have had some hand in education and the upkeep of libraries. As for the belief system itself, we have little clues to go on. It was common for the aristocratic families to have patron deities, whom they worshiped in various ways, like providing patronage to a temple. Besides that, it is hinted that the Punes believed in the afterlife as they placed their eating and drinking utensils in tombs to accompany the dead.

The exact rituals performed by the priests also remain a mystery, but it has been suggested the majority of them were practiced outside of the temples, including prayers, ritual dances, burning incense, and making offerings to the gods at a specially dedicated altar. Apart from offering them various foods, drinks, and animals, it is hinted they also practiced human sacrifice. Many ancient sources mention that yearly sacrifices of children to Baal were made on a sacred site, which historians today call the *tophet*, located south of Byrsa. According to them, those were made to appease the gods. However, the archeological evidence suggests otherwise. Upon closer examination, it seems that most of the remains in the *tophet* were infants and stillborn babies, almost all of whom died of natural causes. That suggests that the *tophet* was nothing more than a children's cemetery.

However, it is possible that they did perform human sacrifices in times of utmost crisis, like a Syracusan invasion or some great pestilence. Some of the Roman and Greek writers actually state such claims, writing that the sacrificed kids were of the ages between six and twelve, sometimes even older. This could be the reason why only a handful of the remains in the *tophet* were of older children. If the sacrifices were real, it's likely they weren't performed at the *tophet* and that the sacrificed children were not related to the people offering them as a tribute, despite what the sources claim. It is also worth noting that *tophets* were also found across several Punic and Phoenician colonies across the Mediterranean.

Remains of the Carthaginian tophet. Source: https://commons.wikimedia.org

The case of child sacrifices showcases the constant issue with Carthaginian history. Most of our accounts have been written by the Greeks and the Romans. This doesn't mean the Punes didn't write about themselves, but rather, as with many other aspects of the Carthaginian civilization, their literary works were lost. As it was mentioned previously, we know some of their authors wrote about agriculture and farming, hinting that others may have written about other aspects of the economy, possibly trade. From the travel logs of Hanno, though they are known to us only from Greek excerpts, it is clear they also wrote about sea voyages and explorations. The question about written histories or annals is still a matter of debate. Some think that historiography wasn't a developed genre in Carthage, explaining the lack of Punic history books. However, others point out that Hannibal left personal accounts of his campaigns in Hera's temple in southern Italy, while in Carthage, an inscription was found that reports on actions taken in Sicily in 406 BCE. This indicates that the Punes did write about at least their military exploits. Coupled with that is the fact that we know they took great pride in their ancestry, meaning they took an interest in family history. That together suggests that the Carthaginians were, in fact, familiar with the historiographical genre and were indeed practicing some form of it. This suggests that Punic histories existed but were not saved.

Other genres are also hinted by Greek and Roman accounts, like philosophy and poetry. However, again, we have little factual evidence about those works. The main reason is the fact that the Romans had little desire to preserve them, proved by the fact that they gave almost all of the Punic libraries to the local African kings in 146. However, through the preserved inscriptions, we know that Carthaginian literary accomplishments were written in what we today call the Punic language. As it's easy to assume, early Carthaginians spoke the Phoenician language. However, over time, they developed their own distinct dialect thanks to the influences of the local Berber population, as well as from their trading partners and immigrants. Nonetheless, they kept using the Phoenician alphabet, which is, in fact, the blueprint for both Latin and Greek alphabets. Like the Phoenicians, the Punes wrote without vowels from right to left in horizontal lines. Thanks to its likeness with other Semitic languages, researchers today can decipher most of it, though there are still many uncertainties and debates about some of the translations of the Punic inscriptions. The Punic language itself survived long after the fall of Carthage, transforming into Neo-Punic, which was spoken in parts of northern Africa until about the 6th century CE.

Unlike the literary works, Carthaginian art has been preserved at least to some degree. Yet there are some limitations to what has been found, as the majority of items were found in graves and temples. This could explain why most of them had religious motifs, though there is no evidence that profane art differed much in that aspect. Regardless of that, their visual arts show a similar path of development as the rest of their culture. The oldest influence was, of course, the old Phoenician style, with common eastern or Mesopotamian motifs, though early on, Egyptian art caught on as well. Somewhat unexpectedly, the Egyptian influence proved to be quite strong and long-lasting. Later on, the Etruscan style also began to permeate Carthaginian art; however, it was the Greeks who became a primary influence in later periods. Ironically, the Greek fad began in the 5th century, after the Punes had looted prosperous Greek cities in Syracuse. The Carthaginian artists reproduced all of these styles, and to the finest level, despite the outdated belief that they mainly imported high-quality art products. However, in some cases, it is hard to determine if an item was locally made or imported. That being said, the Carthaginian artisans and craftsmen weren't just mere copiers of others. In time, they began to merge and blend various styles and motifs to create art pieces unique to the Punic culture.

Among the most commonly found items are small figurines, usually of some goddess or in some cases of Melqart. These were often buried with the deceased or given as offerings in temples. Early types of these statuettes are quite simple; the female figurines have flat-topped heads and cylindrical bodies, while Melqart is posed sitting on a throne with a raised hand in blessing. With the arrival of Greek influences, the figurines were made with Greek clothing and robes. Yet the Punes never made nude statuettes, unlike the Greeks. It is worth noting that these clay figurines were also painted, like in other ancient cultures. Other notable themes for these small sculptures were female figures playing tambourines or flutes. In some cases, there was a blend of influences, such as the winged-depictions of Isis wearing a typical Egyptian wide collar with Greek robes. Other commonly found items are various vessels shaped like animal heads, such as ducks and cows. Most of these were made from clay. However, not all Punic art was static, as shown by figurines of dancing females, usually made in ivory, and a relief of a fully galloping armed horseman, followed by his dog. One of the more distinctively Punic motifs were slightly more abstract faces, usually grinning, which were also found on various statues that were mixed in with the other elements mentioned above.

However, this motif of a grinning face was far more common in clay masks, which the Punes used to ward off evil spirits. These masks are small and not actually made for wearing but were instead usually placed in tombs or hung on walls. With stylized features like ferocious grins and staring eyes, often painted in vivid colors, these votive masks are somewhat unique to the Carthaginians. Another type of mask commonly found is of a smiling woman's face, without any grotesque features, which was more in line with Greek influences. The motif of faces and heads was translated into jewelry as well. A common item among the Carthaginians were necklaces made out of glass beads in the shape of male heads. Those were also colorful, with staring eyes, curly hair, and beards. Besides glass, these beads, as well as other jewelry items, were made out of precious metals and pearls. Other items like earrings, pendants, bracelets, and diadems were commonly decorated with Egyptian motifs of lions, falcons, and lotus blossoms, as well as various gods and more Punic images like palms and eyes. It seems that jewelry was worn by anyone who could afford them, regardless of sex. Amulets of glass paste and semi-precious stones and scarabs were also made with Egyptian symbols and gods, and they were worn for magical protection and as a class symbol. The Greek influence was more prominent in intaglios, small engraved gems, which commonly depicted scenes from Greek mythology.

The Carthaginians also created other decorative objects like bowls, jars, and vases, and more famously painted ostrich eggs. These were ornamented with various geometric forms, palms, and lotus blossoms, commonly in red paint. Similar symbols can be found on metal jewelry boxes, as well as mirror handles, which were sometimes carved from ivory or wood. Of course, besides those, deities were also engraved. The colorful glass was also used to create smaller vessels, usually two-handled, which were commonly used for storing perfumes and ointments. This type of glassware was common across the Mediterranean, but the Carthaginian ones are characterized by dark blue glass adorned with white, yellow, green, and turquoise stripes, colors commonly seen in other Carthaginian art pieces. Among the representations of Carthaginian art are coins as well. Though not meant to be artwork, these often exhibited an impressive artistic quality. The most common motifs were a horse or a horse's head, a palm tree, and the profile of a goddess or god. The goddess was usually Tanit, less commonly Dido or Isis, while the god was typically Melqart, commonly depicted as Heracles. Other less common elements were lions, elephants, or war elephants, as well as warships prows. The latter two were struck by the Barcids in Spain. Notably, the craftsmanship and quality of design worsened with lesser denominations, which were made out of bronze. The style of these coins is clearly based on the Sicilian Greek coins, even though the motifs are distinctively Carthaginian.

A Carthaginian coin with depictions of goddess Tanit and a horse. Source: https://commons.wikimedia.org

On a larger scale, there are a lot of Carthaginian stone stelae preserved in various cemeteries and *tophets*. They were placed above tombs, as markers or possibly altars, and were carved with reliefs of diverse religious natures. The most common symbols depicted were the symbols of Tanit, as well as the sun and crescent moon; there were, of course, also other religious motifs alongside these ones. In some cases, they were engraved with a commemorative inscription. In later periods, the decorations became more complex, once again mixing various styles. One example of that is a stele with a carved Greek Ionian column holding an Egyptian sphinx, with stylized Punic palms above it. By the last century, Carthaginian artists began adorning stelae with animal and human figures, hand motifs, and even in some cases with attempted portraits. At times, instead of stelae, the Punes opted for stone ossuaries or sarcophagi, which were used to preserve the deceased remains. The early ones bore clear Egyptian marks and symbols, with a two-dimensional representation of the departed. With the arrival of the Hellenistic influences, the figures became three-dimensional, combining, in some cases, Egyptian motifs and the Greek style. It's worth noting that not all of the ossuaries were of a full length of a human, and it seems that most, if not all, of them were colored. It is also likely that they were used only by wealthier classes.

Similar development and style can be seen in the Punic architecture as well. Though most of Punic Carthage was destroyed, there are remains of Punic constructions in the Carthaginian colonies, while carvings on stelae and the writing in ancient sources also shed some light on the topic. Common homes were usually built with mud bricks with flat roofs. Usually single storied, some went up to six floors high, at least according to the sources. These simple homes tend to be more evocative of Phoenicia and Egypt than the Greek-Roman world. The temples were similarly flat-roofed, clearly derived from the same eastern traditions. Older ones had geometrical and Egyptian-styled symbols on their entablatures, which were further adorned with columns on their porches. Larger temples also had courtyards for ceremonies. With the arrival of the Hellenistic influences, the columns became fluted, usually decorated with Ionian or Doric capitals, though, in some cases, the Punic palm was also used. However, it was rare to see a clear copy of Greek-styled temples, with the two-sided sloping roof and the triangular facade. The mixing of styles is, however, most evident in mausoleums found across the Punic world. One, about 69 feet (21 meters) high, has three tiers. The first tier is cubic and adorned with a relief of chariots on each vertical face. On top of this is the second square, slightly narrower and decorated with Greek columns. The third tier is also narrower but rests on a pedestal, which has horsemen on its corner. Finally, topping it all off is a low pyramid on another pedestal adorned with sea-nymphs.

The architecture, like all other aspects of the Punic civilization, exhibits their tendency to adopt and adapt the influences of other nations and cultures, using what suited their tastes to create an original and unique creation. Thus, paradoxically, the Punic culture seems to have been derivative of others, as well as being creative and original.

Conclusion

The Carthaginians are usually seen as the glorious yet defeated enemies of the Greeks and Romans, the greedy merchants that would do anything for a coin. However, this guide hopefully counters some of these prejudices that started back in ancient times. Instead of seeing the Carthaginians as a two-dimensional nemesis of two better-known civilizations, this book has tried to present them as a worthy civilization on their own. From humble beginnings, with great explorations and expansion, to their crumbling fall, the Carthaginians created their own path, their own story, and it consisted of more than just soldiers and traders. They created their own art, farmed lands, and wondered about the world around them. They built cities and traveled across the Mediterranean, transporting not only goods and resources but also other more valuable things like ideas and knowledge. They were not afraid to learn from anyone, not even their supposedly sworn enemies. Their openness went in the other direction as well, as their city gates were open for many migrants and new settlers, from wherever they may be from, leading to a cosmopolitanism seen in their entire civilization—a trait that is more reminiscent of the modern global world than ancient societies.

That kind of cosmopolitanism, in a way, makes their entire culture seem like a scrapbook of borrowed ideas and images. Yet it shows how adaptive they really were, as they were often capable of overcoming various hurdles and losses. Not afraid to learn, they accepted when others knew something they didn't. In that, the

Carthaginians were capable of making their own unique creations, something undeniably Punic, yet something so hard to pinpoint precisely, as it shared so much with so many other civilizations. They were, in fact, a truly global culture. Some see this as a negative thing, as if they refused to accept the achievements of others. However, the history of Carthage teaches us that once we stop learning and adapting, we fail. After they were defeated by Rome for the second time, the Carthaginians were not quick enough to adjust and absorb the new Roman ideas, leading to their fall. Yet even though they were finally defeated, their culture continued to live on for centuries, influencing many others to come after them.

Bibliography

A. E. Astin, F. W. Walbank, M. W. Frederiksen And R. M. Ogilvie, *The Cambridge Ancient History: Volume VIII - Rome And the Mediterranean to 133 B.C., Cambridge*, Cambridge University Press, 1989.

A. Salimbeti And R. D'amato, *The Carthaginians 6th-2nd Century BC*, New York, Osprey Publishing, 2014.

Alfred J. Church, *Carthage or the Empire of Africa*, London, T. Fisher Unwin, 1889.

Amy McKenna, *The History of Northern Africa*, New York, Britannica Educational Publishing, 2010.

B. H. Warmington, *Carthage*, London, Trinity Press, 1960.

C. Lopez-Ruiz and B. R. Doak, *The Oxford Handbook of the Phoenician and Punic Mediterranean*, Oxford, Oxford University Press, 2019.

Christa Steinby, *Rome versus Carthage: The War at Sea*, Barnsley, Pen and Sword Maritime, 2014.

Cottrell Leonard, Hannibal: Enemy of Rome. New York, Da Capo Press, 1992.

Dexter Hoyos, *Hannibal's Dynasty Power and Politics in the Western Mediterranean, 247-183 BC, London, Routledge, 2003.*

Dexter Hoyos, *Mastering the West: Rome and Carthage at War*, Oxford, Oxford University Press, 2015.

Dexter Hoyos, *The Carthaginians*, London, Routledge, 2010.

Fernand Braduel, *Memory and the Mediterranean*, New York, Alfred A. Knopf, 2001.

J. D. Fage, *The Cambridge History of Africa Volume I*, Cambridge, Cambridge University Press, 1978.

J. Desmond Clark, *The Cambridge History of Africa Volume II*, Cambridge, Cambridge University Press, 1982.

Josephine Crawley Quinn, *In Search of The Phoenicians*, Princeton, Princeton University Press, 2018.

Phillip C. Naylor, *North Africa: A History from Antiquity to the Present*, Austin, University of Texas Press, 2009.

R. Bosworth Smith, *Carthage and the Carthaginians*, London, Longmans, Green and Co., 1913.

R. Docter, R. Boussoffara and P. ter Keurs, *Carthage: Fact and Myth*, Leiden, Sidestone Press, 2015.

Richard Miles, *Carthage Must Be Destroyed: Rise and Fall of an Ancient Civilization*, New York, Viking Penguin, 2010.

Serge Lancel, *Carthage: A History*, New Jersey, Wiley-Blackwell, 1995.

Free Bonus from Captivating History
(Available for a Limited time)

Hi History Lovers!

Now you have a chance to join our exclusive history list so you can get your first history ebook for free as well as discounts and a potential to get more history books for free! Simply visit the link below to join.

Captivatinghistory.com/ebook

Also, make sure to follow us on Facebook, Twitter and Youtube by searching for Captivating History.

CPSIA information can be obtained
at www.ICGtesting.com
Printed in the USA
LVHW040315140621
690156LV00015B/319

9 781647 486860